The Songs of Paul Simon

as sung by Simon & Garfunkel
and Paul Simon himself, from
"Hey, Schoolgirl" and "The Sound of Silence"
through "Mrs. Robinson,"
"Bridge Over Troubled Water"
and "Mother and Child Reunion"

Alfred A. Knopf
New York

bbi
Big Bells Incorporated
New Jersey
1972

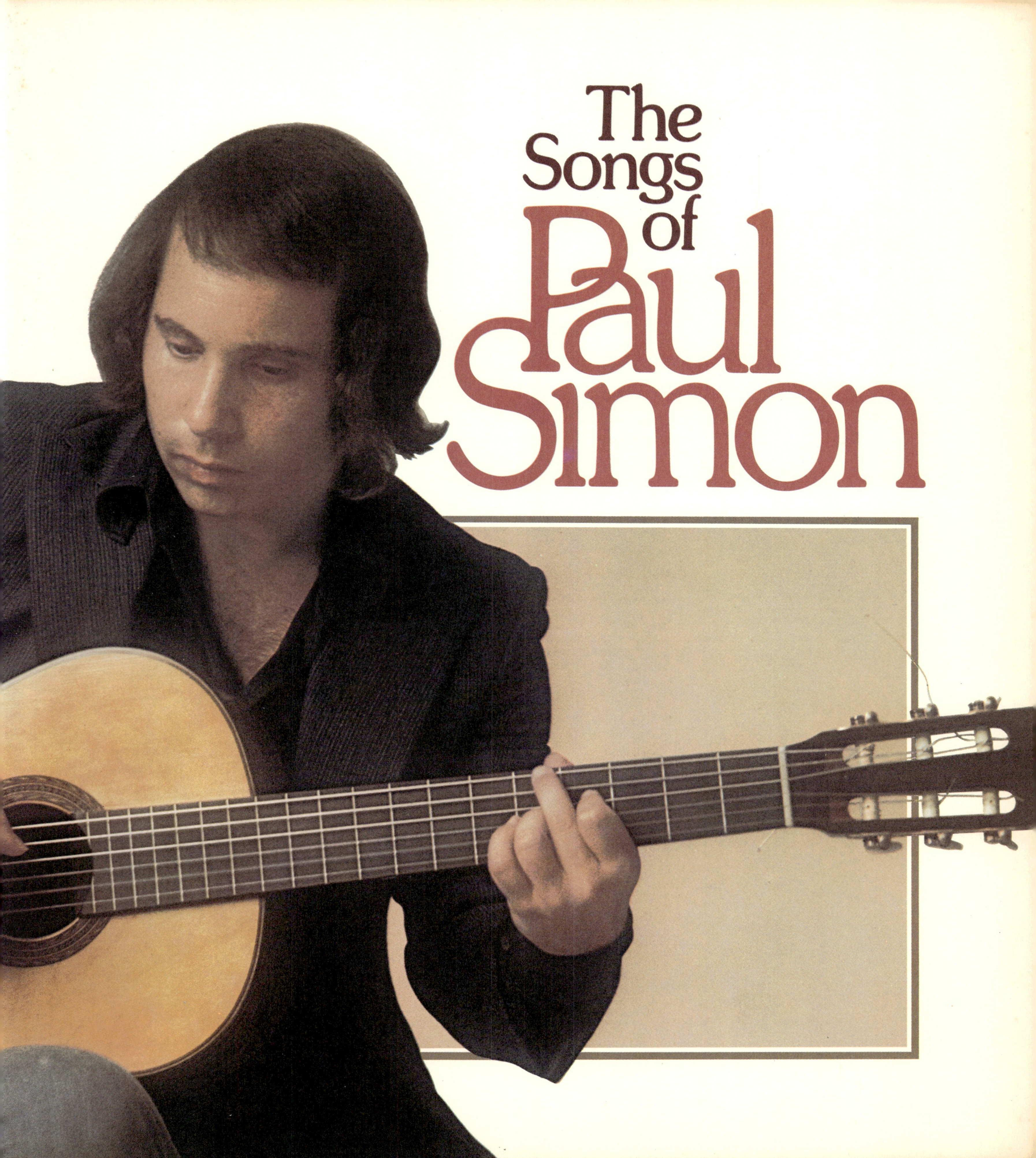
The Songs of Paul Simon

The Songs of Paul Simon

Published on behalf of Paul Simon by Charing Cross Music, Inc.

Published in the United States in association with Alfred A. Knopf, Inc., New York, and simultaneously in Canada by Random House of Canada Limited, Toronto. Distributed by Random House, Inc., New York, and Big Bells Inc., New Jersey.

Library of Congress Cataloging in Publication Data
Simon, Paul, 1941–
The Songs of Paul Simon.

1. Music, Popular (Songs., etc.)—U.S.
M1630.18.S549S62 784'.0924 78-38322
ISBN 0-394-48000-7
ISBN 0-394-70783-4 (pbk)

Manufactured in the United States of America
First Edition

All songs by Paul Simon except: "Hey, Schoolgirl," words and music by Arthur Garfunkel and Paul Simon; "Red Rubber Ball," words and music by Paul Simon and Bruce Woodley; "Scarborough Fair/Canticle," arrangement and original counter melody by Paul Simon and Arthur Garfunkel; "7 o'clock News/Silent Night," narration and arrangement by Paul Simon and Arthur Garfunkel; "El Condor Pasa," musical arrangement by Jorge Milchberg and Daniel Robles, English lyric by Paul Simon; "Hobo's Blues" by Paul Simon and Stephane Grappelli.

With gratitude to the people at Knopf, without whose diligence this book would not have been possible.

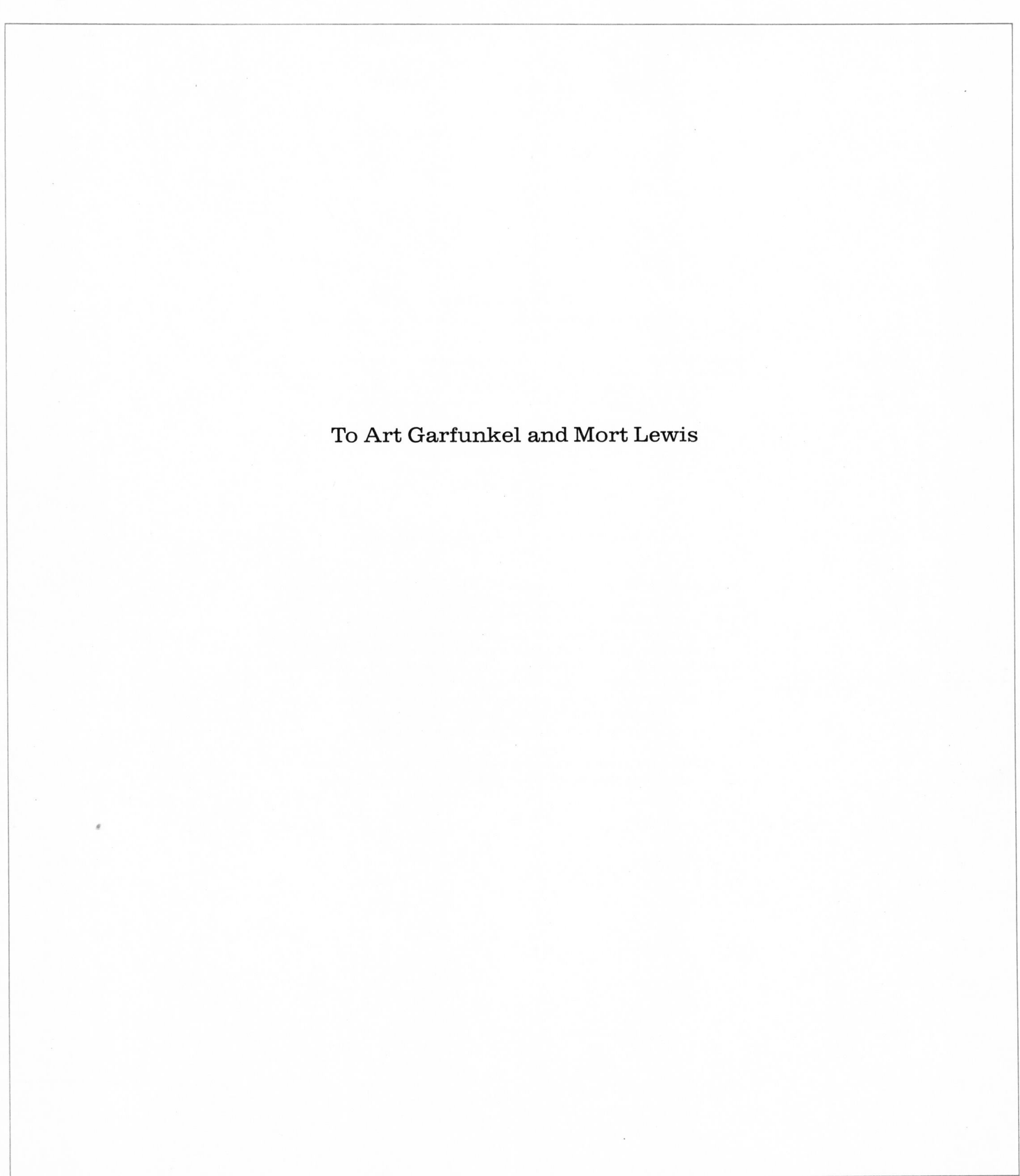

To Art Garfunkel and Mort Lewis

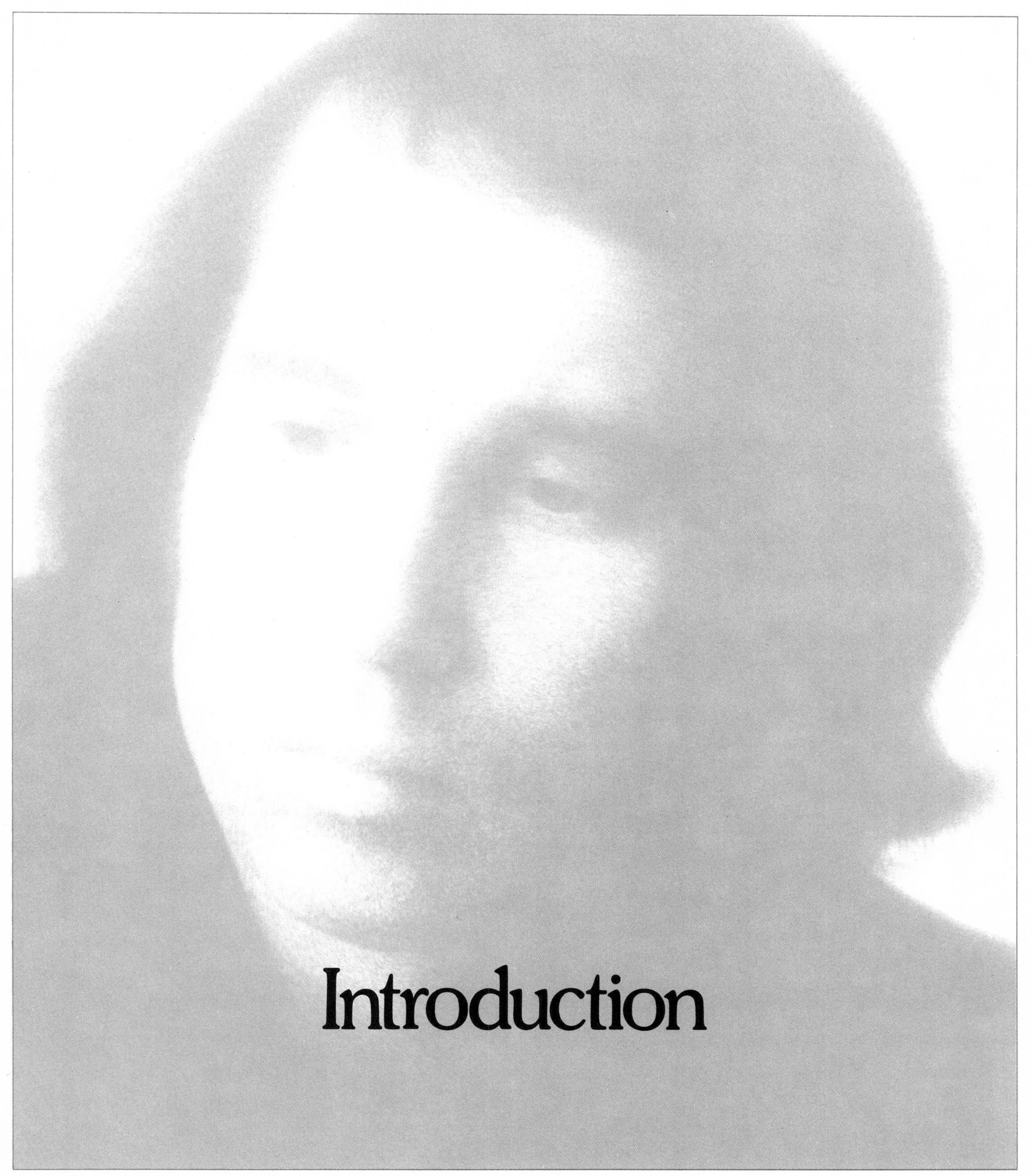

Introduction

I just sit down with a guitar, pick a key, and play. Since the guitar is an instrument more suited to the sharp keys, I usually find myself in C, D, E, F#, G, or A, or their relative minors. I try to vary the keys I play in so that I can avoid that feeling of sameness on a record. I also find it helpful to wander around in keys I'm less familiar with, as this keeps me from repeating the same changes from song to song.

Once I pick a key and start to play, I sing any words that come into my head without trying to make any sense out of them. I tend to sing easy words with a concentration on "oos" and "ah" sounds, which are musically pleasing to me. I also like words beginning with "g's" and "l's" and words that have "t's" and "k's" in them. Sometimes during this stream of consciousness singing, a phrase will develop that has a naturalness and a meaning, in which case I keep it and start to build a song around it. I almost always complete the melody before the lyric. Nevertheless, I think the best songs are those where words and music really come simultaneously. I remember that I wrote the line "like a Bridge Over Troubled Water I will lay me down" at the same moment that I wrote the musical phrase. The rest of the lyrics were written backward from those words. Also the words to the first verse of "The Boxer" came with the melody line; they had a flow to them that made them easy to sing. Consequently I found I had started a song about a "poor boy" who had "squandered (his) resistance/For a pocketful of mumbles." I just tried to make the rest of the lyrics follow as naturally as possible.

Sometimes I finish an entire melody with no lyrics worth keeping, in which case I go into the studio, put down a musical track, go home and take my time over the lyric. The words to "Mother And Child Reunion," "Duncan," and "Peace Like A River" were all written this way. "Cecilia," on the other hand, was recorded on a home tape recorder. We were all sitting around the livingroom, making up rhythms by pounding on a piano bench and hand clapping, and the lyrics and melody were added later to this percussion track. The lyrics were the first words that came to mind—"I'm down on my knees/I'm begging you please"—lines heard in hundreds of songs. They're clichés but then the song really has nothing to say.

"El Condor Pasa" was more complicated. I first heard the melody in Paris in 1965 when it was performed by a group of South American musicians called Los Incas, and I would listen to their recording from time to time, because the melody was so powerful. I wrote a lyric in 1970 and we got permission to use the original recording by Los Incas as our music track.

"Bridge Over Troubled Water" was written on guitar to be played on piano. I never really bothered to work out a guitar part because I knew it should be sung to a gospel piano accompaniment. I got the idea for the lyrics while listening to a Swan Silvertones' recording of "O Mary Don't You Weep." The "sail on silvergirl" verse was written in the studio several weeks after I had completed the first two verses, and I always felt you could tell it was added later as it never really fit the first two verses in style. Also, I couldn't think of another "down" rhyme, so the metaphor "I will lay me down" is discarded in the last verse and "I'm sailing right behind" is substituted. Apart from this weakness, I think "Bridge" is my strongest melody to date, even if not the best lyric.

I divide the sixty or seventy real songs I've written into these categories: the early ones like "The Sound Of Silence," "Leaves That Are Green," "Sparrow," and those on the **Wednesday Morning, 3 A.M.** album. Of this group, clearly "The Sound Of Silence" is the strongest. Next are the songs written while I was living in England, around 1965. These include "Homeward Bound," "Blessed," "April Come She Will," and "A Most Peculiar Man." Then in late 1966 and early 1967 I hit a dry patch, and the songs and recordings of that period—like "A Hazy Shade Of Winter," "The Dangling Conversation," "At The Zoo," and "The Big Bright Green Pleasure Machine"—don't seem so great to me now. In fact, I don't think I regained my stride until about the time of **Bookends** in 1968. "America," for instance, is a good "road song," not unlike "Homeward Bound" or "Papa Hobo." And I like "The Boxer" in the **Bridge** album. Some of the songs which are favorites of mine—like "Homeward Bound," "Blessed," and "A Most Peculiar Man"—are not necessarily my best, it's just that they seem to me innocent and young (and a little pretentious). I also like "Mrs. Robinson"—or "Ms. Robinson," if you prefer.

Of my more recent songs, I like "Mother And Child Reunion" because of the Reggae band on the recording and the strange lyric about death. The title, by the way, comes from a dish I had in a Chinese restaurant. It was boiled eggs and fried chicken and was very good. I also like "Run That Body Down." Musically it derives from a Bach prelude I was playing, and lyrically it makes it for me because I like the idea of a song about taking care of your health. I was reading a lot of Adelle Davis at the time.

This book has all the songs I've written since 1963 with the exception of two really bad ones I wouldn't want to look at, three songs that E. B. Marks Music wouldn't give permission to reprint, and a new song I haven't had a chance to record.

I think my next songs will be better. —Paul Simon

Photo Credits

Photographer	Page
Unknown	I
Steve Weiner	II-III
Steve Weiner	IX
Unknown	17
Unknown	17
Henry Parker	19
Unknown	32
Henry Parker	33
Guy Webster	35
Guy Webster	38
Unknown	52
Don Hunstien	63
Don Hunstien	69
Peter Powell/Abbott Mills	70-71
Bob Cato	73
Don Hunstien	74-75
Susan J. Smith	83
WTOP Radio	102
Don Hunstien	120-121
Richard Avedon	123
Steve Shapiro	124
Unknown	125
Richard Avedon	146-147
Don Hunstien	152
Bob Cato	156
Peter Powell/Abbott Mills	178-179
Peter Powell/Abbott Mills	181
Peggy Simon	182-183
Nosaki	184
Don Hunstien	205
Unknown	214
Unknown	231
Peter Powell/Abbott Mills	232-233
Peter Powell/Abbott Mills	234
Peter Powell/Abbott Mills	235
Peggy Simon	237
Teresa Alfieri	268
Steve Weiner	269
Don Hunstien	270-271
Peggy Simon	272
Ronnie Baldwin	289
Unknown	301
Bruno of Hollywood	302-303
Unknown	304-305
Guy Webster	306
Don Hunstien	307
Guy Webster	308
Bob Cato	309
Paul & Artie—Unknown	310-311
Bridge—DeWys Inc.	310-311
Don Hunstien	313
Unknown	314-315
Don Hunstien	316
Don Hunstien	319
Chas. B. Slackman (artist)	320
Peter Powell/Abbott Mills	322
Peter Powell/Abbott Mills	323
Don Hunstien	324
UPI (wirephoto)	325
Steve Weiner	331

Designed by Charles Schmalz

Hey, Schoolgirl

G
C
G
D7
to say, "Who-bop-a-loo-chi-bop, let's meet af-ter school at
G
1.2.
C
G
three."
1. She said, "Hey, babe, but there is one thing more,
2. She said, "Hey, babe, I got-ta lot to do,
D7
G
C
My school is o-ver at a half-past four,
It takes me ho-urs till my home-work's thru,
May-be when we're old-er, then
Some-day we'll go stead-y, so
G
D7
G
we can date, Ooh, let's wait!"
don't you fret, Ooh, not yet!"

3.
C
G
3. Then she turned a-round to me with that gleam in her eye,
D7
G
She said, "I'm sor-ry if I passed you by, I'm gon-na
C
G
D7
skip my home-work, gon-na cut my class,
Bug out of here
G
G
D7
G
E♭
C
real fast." Hey, School-girl in the sec-ond row,

G
D7
Now we're go - in' stead - , y, hear the words that I want_ you to
G
Eb
C
C
know.
Well, it's "Who - bop - a - loo - chi - bop,
G
D7
G
you're mine,
I knew it all the time."
Fade out
D7
G
Who - bop - a - loo - chi - bop,
hah, you're mine.

A Church Is Burning

Eb Gm Fm Ab
like hands that are pray - ing a - glow in the
Bb Fm7 Bb Eb Ab Gm Fm
sky Like hands that are pray - ing the fire is
Eb Ab Eb Bb7 Eb Bb
say - ing, "You can burn down my church - es but I shall be free."
Eb Bb Eb Bb Eb
Verse:
Fm
Three hood-ed men thru the

E♭
Fm
E♭
back-roads did creep Torch-es in their hands while the vil-lage lies a-
A♭
Fm
E♭
D♭
E♭
sleep Down to the church where just hours be - fore
A♭
Fm
E♭
A♭
Fm
E♭
A♭
B♭
voic - es were sing - ing and hands were beat - ing and say - ing I
E♭
B♭7
E♭
won't be a slave an - y more. And A

Chorus:
Eb
Bb
Ab
Eb
Church Is Burn - - - - - - - - ing
Ab
Bb
Eb
Bb
Eb
the flames rise high - er like
Gm
Fm
Ab
Bb
hands that are pray - ing a - glow in the sky
Fm7
Bb
Eb
Ab
Gm
Fm
Eb
Like hands that are pray - ing the fire is say - ing, "You can

Ab
Eb
Bb7
Eb
Bb
Eb
Bb
burn down my church-es but I shall be free."
Eb
Bb
Eb
Verse:
Fm
3
Eb
2. Three hood-ed men, their hands lit the
3. A church is more than just tim - ber and
3
Fm
Eb
spark Then they fad - ed in the night and they van-ished in the dark And in the
stone And free-dom is a dark road when you're walk-ing it a - lone; But the
Ab
Fm
Eb
Ab
Fm
Eb
cool light of morn - ing there's noth - ing that re - mains But the
fu - ture is now and it's time to take a stand So the

Ab
Eb
Bb7
Eb
1 Eb
2. Eb
D.S. al
ash-es of a bi-ble and a can of ker-o-sene. And A And a
lost bells of free-dom can ring out in my land.
Ab
Fm
Eb
Cm
burn down my church - es But
Ab
Bb
Ab
Fm
I shall be
Eb
Bb
Eb
Fm
Eb
Bb
Eb
free.

You Don't Know Where Your Interest Lies

Cm Bb Cm
What you think is - n't al - ways true. Don't try to de - bate
Bb Cm Bb Cm
me, You should know that I'm wom - an - ly wise.
Bb Cm
Still you try to ma - nip - u - late me, You Don't Know Where Your
Bb Ab Fm7 Gm Ab Gm Bdim
In - ter - est Lies. No, You Don't Know Where Your

To next strain
Fine
Cm
Ddim
G (omit3rd)
C (omit 3rd, add 9)
Bb
Ab
In - ter - est Lies. (Spoken) You don't begin to comprehend.
You're just a game that I like to play,
You may think that we're friends all right, but
I won't let friend - ship get in my way,
No,

Fm7 Gm A♭ Gm Bdim Cm C (omit 3rd, add 9)
I won't let friend - ship get in my way.
Slowly
A♭m7 G♭m7 C♭ F♭ C♭
In - di - ca - tions in - di - cate run - nin' the same riff will turn
mp
B♭ F♭ C♭
you a - round, Ob - vious - ly you're goin' to blow it, But
D♭m7 E♭m E G♭
With a moving beat (as before)
Cm
you don't know it.
mf

D.S. al fine

Red Rubber Ball

B♭
Gm
Cm
Dm
star - fish in the sea. If I nev - er hear your name a - gain it's
that's the life you live. Sto - len min - utes of your time were
near - ly at an end. I bought my tick - et with my tears, that's
E♭
D7
Chorus:
Gm
all the same to me.
all you had to give.
all I'm gon - na spend.
And I think it's gon - na be all right.
Cm
F
Yeah, the worst is o - ver, Now the morn - ing sun is shin - ing like a
E♭
B♭
Gm
F7
Fine(after 3rd Chorus)
B♭
Red Rub-ber Ball.
(3.) The

WEDNESDAY MORNING, 3 A.M.

The Sound of Silence

Dm
F
C
mains with - in The Sound Of
Dm
Dm
C
Si - lence.
(2.) In rest - less dreams I walked a - lone
(3.) And in the nak - ed light I saw
mp (Melody)
Dm
F
nar - row streets of cob - ble - stone, 'Neath the ha - lo of a
ten thou - sand peo - ple, may - be more. Peo - ple talk - ing with - out
B♭
F
B♭
F
street lamp, I turned my col - lar to the cold and damp
speak - ing, peo - ple hear - ing with - out lis - ten - ing

B♭
F
When my eyes were stabbed_ by the flash of a ne - on light that split the
Peo - ple writ - ing songs_ that voi - ces nev - er share and no one
Dm
F
C
Dm
night and touched The Sound Of Si - lence._
dare dis - turb The Sound Of Si - lence._
Dm
C
Dm
(4.) "Fools!" said I, "You do not know si - lence like a can - cer grows."
mf
F
B♭
F
"Hear my words that I might teach you,_ Take my arms that I might

B♭
F
B♭
reach you."
But my words like si - lent rain- drops
F
Dm
F
C
fell,
and ech- oed
in the wells of
Dm
C
si - lence.
(5.) And the peo - ple bowed and prayed
Dm
F
to the ne - on god they made.
And the sign flashed out its

Bb F Bb F
warn - ing. In the words that it was form - ing,
Bb
And the signs said "The words of the proph - ets are writ - ten on the sub - way
F Dm F
walls and ten - e - ment halls" And whis - per'd in The
poco a poco dim.
mp
C Dm
Sounds Of Si - lence.
poco a poco ritard.
(Melody)
p
pp

Sparrow

Moderately
mp
Gm
F
1. Who will
2. Who will
3. Who will
4. Who will
love a lit - tle Spar - row who's trav - eled
love a lit - tle Spar - row and who will
take pit - ty in his heart, And who will
love a lit - tle Spar - row? Will no one

Eb
F
far and cries for rest?
speak a kind - ly word?
feed a starv - ing spar - row?
write her eu - lo - gy?
Gm
C
"Not I," said the oak tree,
"Not I," said the swan,
"Not I," said the gold - en wheat,
"I will," said the earth,
F
Dm
"I won't share my branch - es with
"The en - tire i - dea is
"I would if I could but I
"For all I've cre - a - ted re -

C
F
no spar - row's nest,
And my blank - et of
ut - ter - ly ab - surd,
I'd be laughed at and
can - not I know,
I need all my
turns un - to me,
From dust were ye

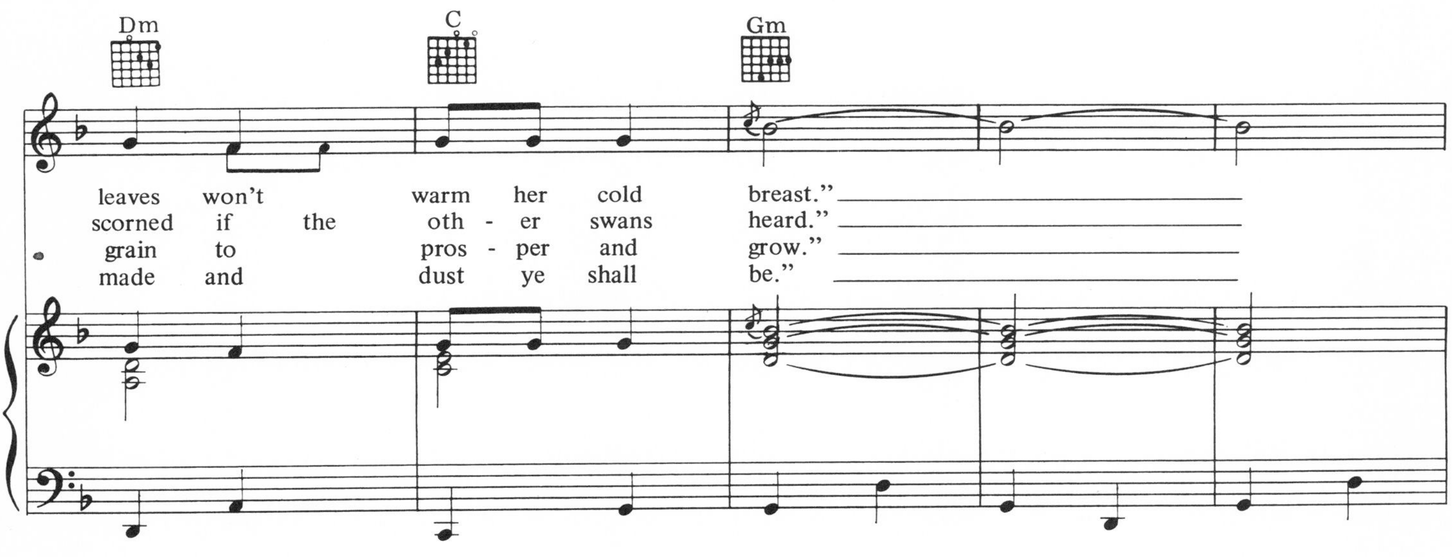
Dm
C
Gm
leaves won't warm her cold breast."
scorned if the oth - er swans heard."
grain to pros - per and grow."
made and dust ye shall be."

1.2.3.
4.
3. And
molto rall.

Wednesday Morning, 3 A.M.

Moderately bright

Am
F
Gm
love, ___ As she lies here be - side me a -
heav - y, ___ And I watch as her breasts gent - ly
C
F
sleep with the night, And her hair, in a
rise, gent - ly fall, For I know with the
Dm
B♭
Am
fine mist floats on my pil - low, ___ Re -
first light of dawn I'll be leav - ing, ___ And to -
F
Gm
B♭
C
flect - ing the glow of the win - ter moon -
night will be all I have left to re -

F
Gm
light.
call.
F
1.
2.
2. She is
3. Oh,
(4. My)
F
Dm
B♭
Am
what have I done, Why have I done it,
life seems un - real, my crime an il - lu - sion,
F
Gm
C
I've com - mit - ted a crime, I've brok - en the law,
A scene bad - ly writ - ten in which I must play,

F
Dm
B♭
Am
For twen - ty - five dol - lars and piec - es of sil - ver,
Yet I know as I gaze at my young love be - side me,
F
1. Gm
B♭
C
I held up and robbed a hard liq - uor
The morn - ing is
F
Gm
F
store.
4. My
2. Gm
B♭
C
just a few hou - - rs a -

F
Gm
F
way.
rit.
p

SOUNDS OF SILENCE

I Am A Rock

Slowly
mp
C
F
mf
1. A win - ter's day In a deep and dark De - cem - ber; I am a - lone,
2. walls, A fort - ress deep and might-y, That none may pen - e -
3. love; But I've heard the word be - fore; It's sleep - ing in my mem - o -
4. books And my po - e - try to pro - tect me; I am shield - ed in my ar -
C
Dm
G7
F

C
Dm7
Em7
Dm7
Em7
Gaz - ing from my win - dow To the streets be - low On a
trate. I have no need of friend-ship; Friend-ship caus - es pain. It's
ry, I won't dis - turb the slum-ber of feel - ings that have died. If I
mour, Hid - ing in my room, Safe with - in my womb. I
Dm
F
G
F
C
F
fresh - ly fal - len si - lent shroud of snow.
laugh - ter and it's lov - ing I dis - dain.
nev - er loved I nev - er would have cried.
touch no one and no one touch - es me.
I Am A Rock, I am an is -
f
G7
1.2.3.
C
Am
land.
4.
C
Dm7
G7
2. I've built
3. Don't talk of
4. I have my land.
And a rock feels no
mf
mf

C
Dm7
G7
C
pain; And an is - land nev - er cries.
p

Leaves That Are Green

A7 D C G Em7 A7 D
on ___ write ___ And the Leaves That Are Green ___ turn to brown, ___
Bm
And they with-er with the wind, ___ And they
Em7 A7 1. D 2. A7 D
crum-ble in your hand. ___ 2. Once my heart was 3. I threw a
Em A7 D G C D
peb - ble in a brook And watched the rip - ples run a - way ___
lo, Hel - lo, Good - bye, Good - bye, Good - bye, Good - bye, Good - bye, ___

G
A7
Em7 A7
D
C
G Em7
And they nev - er made a sound.
That's all there is.
And the Leaves That Are Green
A7
D
turned to brown,
Bm
And they with-er with the wind,
Em7
A7
D
D.S. al
And they crum-ble in your hand.
4. Hel - lo, Hel -
Coda
D
Bm
brown.
A7
A

Blessed

Fairly fast
D
G
F♯m
Em
D
G
Bless - ed are the meek for they shall in - her - it.
Bless - ed is the land and the king - - - dom.
Bless - ed are the stained glass, win - dow pane glass.
Bless - ed is the lamb whose blood
Bless - ed is the man whose soul
Bless - ed is the church ser - vice makes

F♯m
Em
D
G
flows.
be - longs to.
me ner - vous.
D
C
Bless - ed are the sat up - on, Spat up - on, Rat -
Bless - ed are the meth drink - ers, Pot sel - lers, Il -
Bless - ed are the pen - ney rookers, Cheap hook-ers, groov -
G
D
- - - ted on.
lu - - sion dwell - ers.
- - - y look - ers.
O
F♯m
Em
G
D
Lord, Why have you for - sak - en me?

1.
Am
I got no place to go,
Bm
I've walked a - round So - ho
Am
for the last night or so
Bm
Ah, but it does - n't mat - ter,
Am
no.
D
D.C.
2.
Am
3
My words trick-le down,
3

Bm
Am
like a wound that I have no in - ten - tion to
D
D.C.
3. Am
heal.
I
Bm
Am
I have tend - ed my own gar - den much too
D
No chord
long.
Repeat and fade

Kathy's Song

Moderately
p
G
C
G
1. I hear the driz - zle of the rain
2. And from the shel - ter of my mind
3. My mind's dis - tract - ed and dif - fused
Am
Em
C
Bm7
Like a mem - o - ry it falls
Through the win - dow of my eyes
My thoughts are man - y miles a - way

G
Bm
G
C
Soft and warm con - tin - u - ing
I gaze be - yond the rain - drenched streets
They lie with you when you're a - sleep
Am
Em
D
Tap - ping on my roof and
To Eng - land where my heart
And kiss you when you start your
G
C
G
G
C
G
walls.
lies.
day.
G
C
G
4. And a song I was writ - ing is left un - done
5. And so you see I have come to doubt
6. And as I watch the drops of rain

Am
Em
C
Bm7
I don't know why I spend my time
All that I once held as true
Weave their wear - y paths and die
G
Bm
G
C
writ - ing songs I can't be - lieve
I stand a - lone with - out be - liefs
I know that I am like the rain
Am
Em
D
G
C
With words that tear and strain to rhyme.
The on - ly truth I know is you.
There but for the grace of you go I.
G
G
C
1.2.
G
3.
G
C
G

Somewhere They Can't Find Me

D7
Gm
sleep with the night. Her hair in a
brok - en the law. While you were here
which I must play. And though it puts me up tight to
F
fine mist floats on my pil - low, Re -
sleep - ing and just dream - ing of me, I
leave you, I know it's not right to leave you, When
Gm
E♭
D7
Chorus:
flect - ing the glow of the win - ter moon - light.
held up and robbed a liqu - or store
morn - ing is just a few hours a - way.
But I've got to

B♭
Gm
Gm
F
creep down the al - ley way,
fly down the high - way,
Gm
C
Gm
E♭
Be - fore they come to catch me I'll be
Gm9
B♭
C
Gm
gone.
Some - where
They Can't Find Me.

1.2.
3.
C
Gm
2. Oh
3. Oh my
Repeat and fade

Richard Cory

A
G
spread his wealth a - round Born in - to so - ci -
Cor - y at a show. And the ru - mor of his part
thanked him ver - y much, So my mind was filled with won-
- e - ty, a bank - er's on - ly child, He had
- ies and the or - gies on his yacht! Oh, he
- der when the eve - ning head - lines read: "Rich - ard
Dm
C
F
A
ev - 'ry - thing a man could want: pow - er, grace and
sure - ly must be hap - py with ev - 'ry - thing he's
Cor - y went home last night and put a bul - let through his
F
F
Dm
style.
got.
head."
But I work in his fac - to - ry

G
And I curse the life I'm liv - in' And I curse my pov - er - ty And I wish
F
Dm
that I could be, Oh, I wish that I could be, Oh, I wish
G
1.2.
Dm
that I could be Rich-ard Cor - y.
3.
Dm
2. The
3. He Cor - y.

A Most Peculiar Man

D
G
A7
stairs from him
She said he was A Most Pe - cul - iar
D
Man.
He was A
Most Pe - cul - iar Man.
Em
He lived all a - lone with - in a house, With - in a room,

A7
D
G
A7
within himself,
A Most Peculiar
D
Man.
He had no
friends,
he seldom spoke
And
Em
no one in turn
ever spoke to him,
'Cause he wasn't friendly and he

A7
D
G
did - n't care
And he was - n't like them.
Oh, no!
He was A
A7
D
Most Pe - cul - iar Man.
He died last
Sat - ur - day.
He
Em
turned on the gas and he went to sleep
With the win - dows closed so he'd
3

nev - er wake up To his si - lent world and his tin - y room; And
A7
Mis - sus Rior - don says he has a broth - er some- where Who should be
D
G
A7
no - ti - fied soon. And all the peo - ple said, "What a
D
Bm
G
A7
D
shame that he's dead, But was - n't he A Most Pe - cul - iar Man?"

April Come She Will

Am
Em
G
C
G
arms a - gain.
to her flight.
G
C
G
C
G
C
G
Am
Em
Au - gust, die she must, The au-tumn winds blow chil-
Fmaj7
Em
C
D
G
Em
- ly and cold; Sep - tem - ber I'll re - mem - ber.
Am
Em
D
G
A love once new has now grown old.
p

We've Got A Groovy Thing Goin'

G
I just could - n't be - lieve it, I just could - n't be -
I nev - er ran a - round, I nev - er ran a -
No, no, no, no, no, no, no, no, No, no, no, no,
G7
F
lieve it.
round.
no, no, no.
Oh, ba - by, ba - by, You must be out of your
Dm
Bb
mind. Do you know what you're kick - in' a - way?

A
Dm
We've got a groov - y thing go - in', ba - by,
A
1.2.
Dm
We've got a groov - y thing.
A
tacet
2. I nev - er done you no
3. There's some-thin' you ought to
3. Repeat and fade
Dm
A
We've got a groov - y thing go - in', ba - by, We've got a groov - y thing.

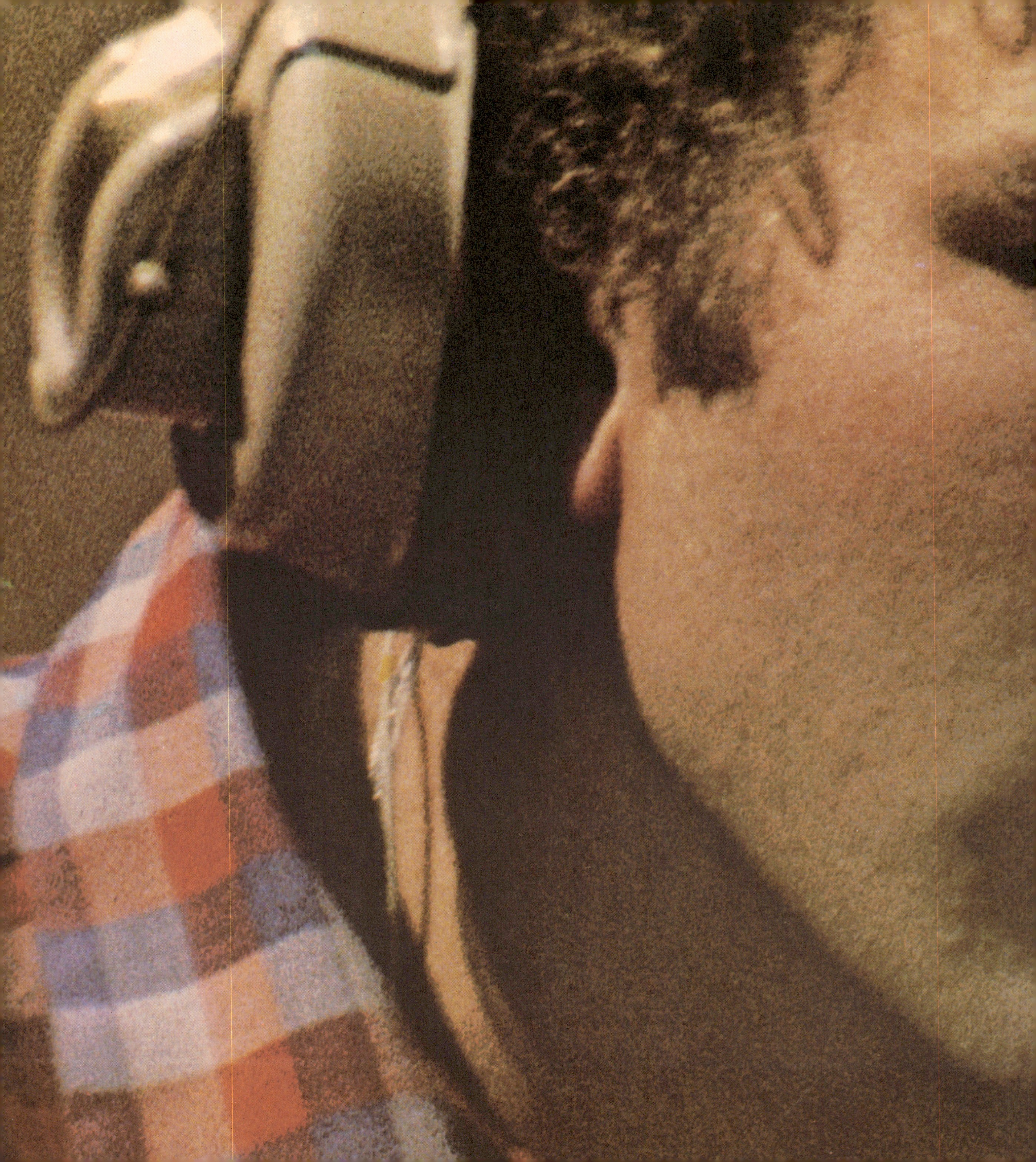

PARSLEY, SAGE, ROSEMARY AND THYME

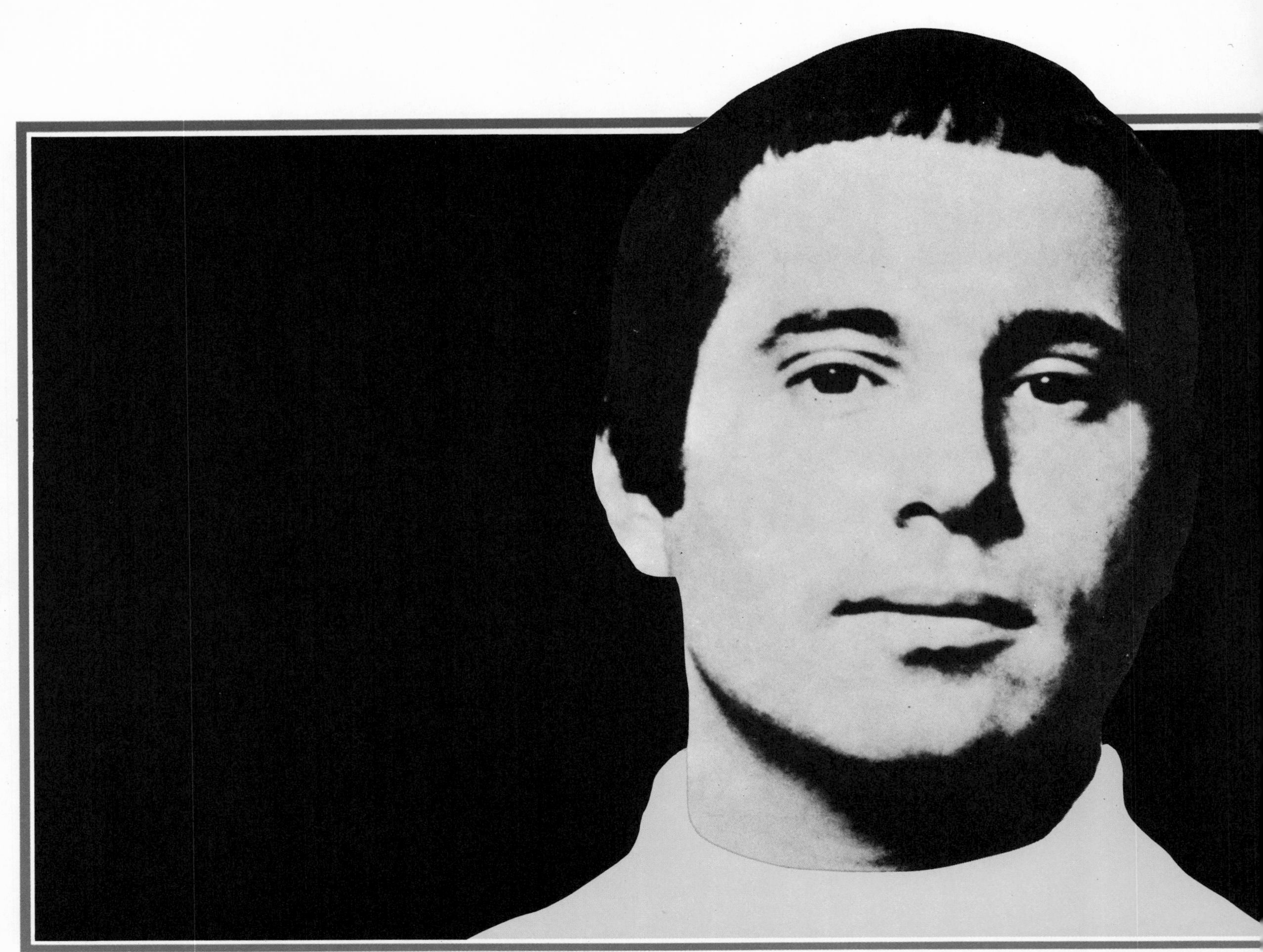

Scarborough Fair/Canticle

Em
thyme.
Re - mem - ber
G
F♯m
Em
D
me to one who lives there.
Em
D
Em
D
Em
D
Ahead to next strain
Em
She once was a true love of mine.
Em
Fine
D
Em
mine.
rit.
p

Em
D
Em
D
Em
On the side of a hill in the deep for - est
On the side of a hill a sprink-ling of
War bel - lows blaz - ing in scar - let bat -
Tell her to make me a cam - bric shirt:
Tell her to find me an a - cre of land:
Tell her to reap it with a sick - le of leath - er:
G
Em
G
A
Em
green.
leaves.
tal - ions.
Trac - ing of spar - row on
Wash - es the grave with
Gen - er - als or - der their
Pars - ley, sage, rose - mar - y and thyme;
Pars - ley, sage, rose - mar - y and thyme;
Pars - ley, sage, rose - mar - y and thyme;
G
F♯m
Em
snow - crest - ed brown.
sil - ver - y tears.
sol - diers to kill.
Blan - kets and
A sol - dier
And to fight for a
With - out no seams nor nee - dle
Be - tween the salt wa - ter and the sea
And gath - er it all in a bunch of

D
Em
D
Em
D
Em
D
bed - clothes the child of the moun - tain.
cleans and po - lish -es a gun.
cause they've long a - go for - got - ten.
work,
strands,
heath - er,
Then she'll be a true love of
Then she'll be a true love of
Then she'll be a true love of
1.2.
Em
Sleeps un - a - ware of the clar - i - on call.
mine.
mine.
3.
Em
D.S. al Fine
mine.

Patterns

Brightly
mp
Dm
F
Dm
1. The night sets soft - ly with the hush of fall - ing leaves, Cast - ing
2. (Up a) nar - row flight of stairs in a nar - row lit - tle room, As I
3. (From the) mo - ment of my birth to the in - stant of my death, There are
4. (And the) pat - tern still re - mains on the wall where dark - ness fell, And it's

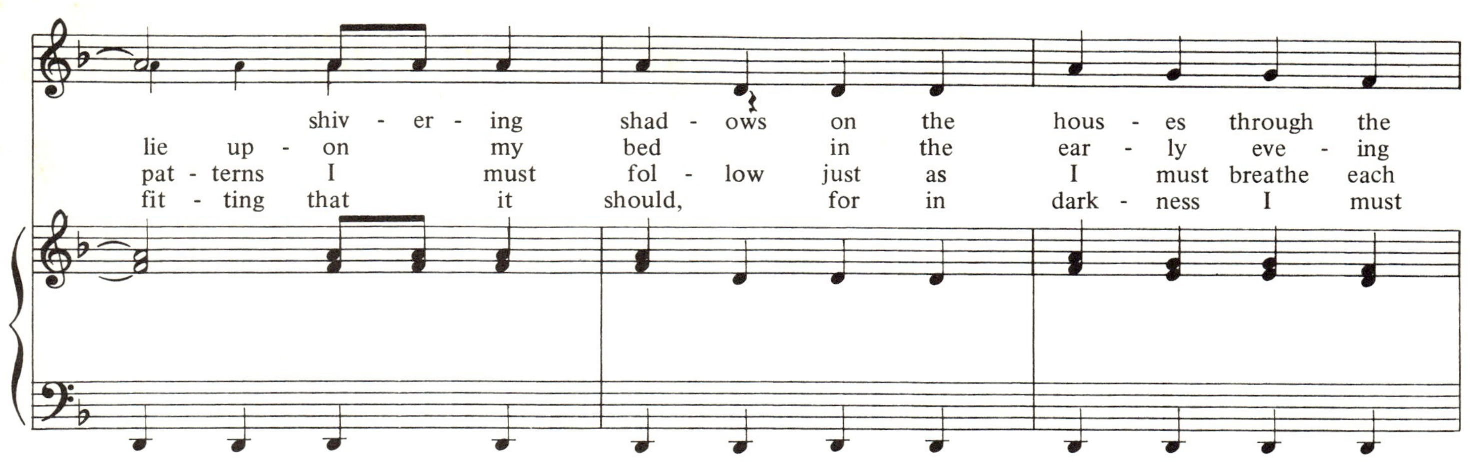
shiv - er - ing shad - ows on the hous - es through the
lie up - on my bed in the ear - ly eve - ing
pat - terns I must fol - low just as I must breathe each
fit - ting that it should, for in dark - ness I must

C
trees, And the
gloom. Im -
breath. Like a
dwell. Like the

Dm
light from the street lamp paints a pat - tern on my
paled on my wall my eyes can dim - ly
rat in a maze the path be - fore me
col - or of my skin, or the day that I grow

F
Dm
wall, Like the
see The
lies, And the
old, My

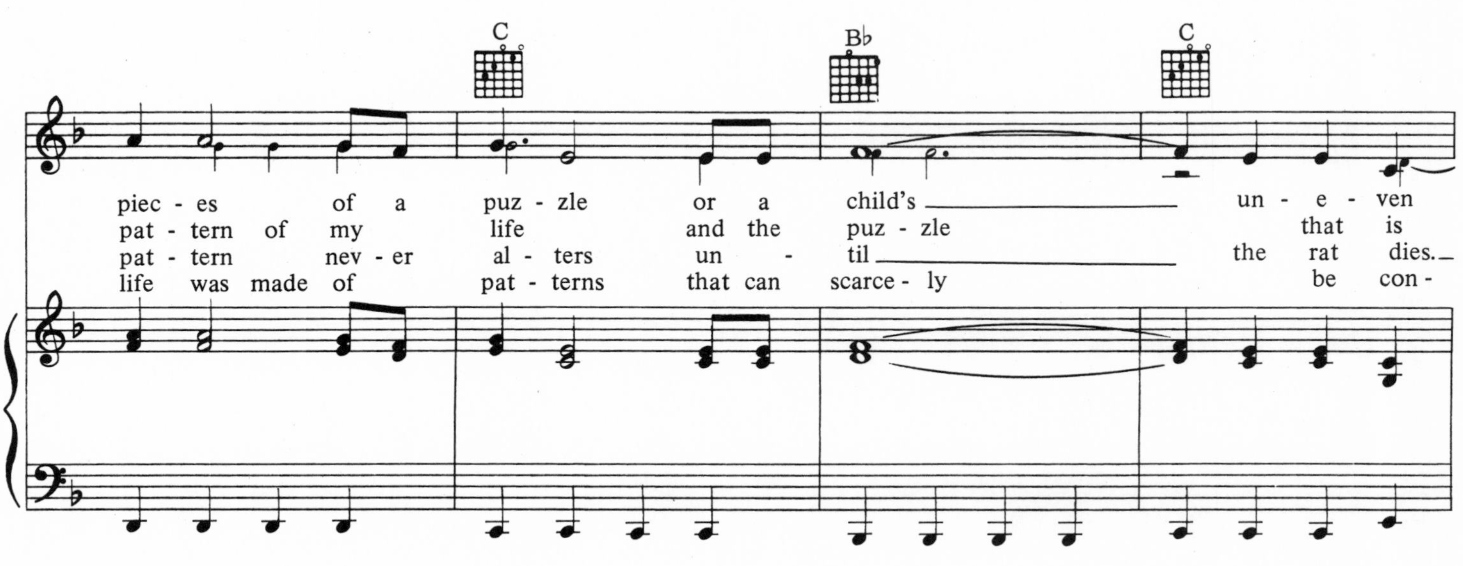
C
B♭
C
piec - es of a puz - zle or a child's un - e - ven
pat - tern of my life and the puz - zle that is
pat - tern nev - er al - ters un - til the rat dies.
life was made of pat - terns that can scarce - ly be con -

Dm
1.2.3.
4.
scrawl.
me.
trolled.
2. Up a
3. From the
4. And the
rall.
p

Cloudy

Rubato
Tempo
D
1. Cloud - y The sky is
2. Cloud - y My thoughts are
Gmaj7
G
grey and white and Cloud - y, Some-times I think it's hang - in'
scat-tered and they're Cloud - y, They have no bor-ders, no
D
Dmaj7
Ddim
A7
F♯m
down on me. And it's a hitch-hike a hun-dred miles.
bound - a - ries. They ech - o and they swell.

84

A
Bm
E
I'm a rag - a - muf - fin child. Point - ed fin - ger - paint - ed
From Tol - stoi to Tink - er Bell. Down from Berke - ley to Car -
E7
A
A7
smile. I left my shad - ow wait - in' down the
mel. Got some pic - tures in my pock - et and a
1. F♯m
A7
2. F♯m
A7
D
road for me a while. kill, Hey sun - shine
lot of time to
DMaj7
Gsus
G
I have - n't seen you in a long time. Why don't you

D
DMaj7
Ddim
A7
show your face and bend my mind?
These clouds stick to the
F♯m
A
Bm
sky like a floating - ing ques - tion, why?
And they
E
E7
A
lin - ger there to die.
They don't know where they're
A7
F♯m
A7
D
go - ing, and, my friend, nei - ther do I,
Cloud - y,
Repeat and fade out
G
Cloud - y.

Homeward Bound

Dm
Bb
On a tour of one night stands my suit-case and gui-tar in hand and ev-'ry stop is neat-ly planned for a po-et and a one man band.
And each town looks the same to me, the mov-ies and the fac-tor-ies and ev-'ry strang-er's face I see re-minds me that I long to be,
But all my words come back to me in shades of me-di-oc-ri-ty like emp-ti-ness in har-mon-ny I need some-one to com-fort me.
C
G7
C
Chorus:
C
F
C
Home-ward Bound, I wish I was,

F
C
Home - ward Bound.
Home where my thought's
Dm C B♭ F C Dm C B♭ F C
es - cap - ing, Home where my mu - sic's play - ing, Home where my love
Dm C B♭ F G7 C
1.2. C
3. C Cmaj7
lies wait - ing si - lent - ly for me.
3. To -
C7 C F C
Si - lent - ly for me.

The Big Bright Green Pleasure Machine

C
cav - i - ties than theirs? Do
bus' - ness world a drag? Did your
than a rub - ber ball? Are you

D
all the hip - pies seem to get the jump on you?
boss just men - tion that you'd bet - ter shop a - round
wor - ried 'cause your girl friend's just a lit - tle late?

C
Do you sleep a - lone when oth - ers sleep in pairs?
to find your - self a more pro - duc - tive bag?
Are you look - ing for a way to chuck it all?

B♭
Well, there's no need to com - plain, We'll e -
Are you wor - ried and dis - tressed? Can't
We can end your dai - ly strife at a
A
lim - i - nate your pain. We can
seem to get no rest? Put our
rea - son - a - ble price. You've seen it
G
neu - tral - ize your brain.
prod - uct to the test.
ad - ver - tised in 'Life.'
A
You'll feel just fine now.
G
F
Buy a Big Bright Green

C
1.
D
Pleas - ure Ma - chine!
2. Do
2. To Next Strain
Fine
D
chine!
chine!
Fade out
A
G
You bet - ter hur - ry up and or - der one.
Our
E
A
D.S. al Fine
lim - it - ed sup - ply is ver - y near - ly gone.
Do you

A Simple Desultory Philippic

(Or How I Was Robert McNamara'd Into Submission)

Eb
F
G
Bea - tled till I'm blind.
I been
I want to pay.
And I
C
C7
F
Ayn Rand - ed, near - ly brand - ed com - mu - nist, 'cause I'm
learned the truth from Len - ny Bruce, And all my wealth won't
1.
G
left - hand - ed, That's the hand I use, well, nev - er
buy me health,
C
mind!
I been
2.
G
So I smoke a

C
pint of tea a day.
C
(Spoken) I knew a man, his brain so
Background for recitation
F
G
small, He couldn't think of nothin' at all. He's not the same as you
C
F
and me. He doesn't dig poetry. He's so un - hip that when you say

G
C
Dylan, He thinks you're talkin' 'bout Dylan Thomas, whoever he was.
F
G
The man ain't got no culture, But it's al—
G
C
right, ma, Everybody must get stoned.
C
(Sung) I been Mick Jag-gered, been sil-ver dag-gered.

F
Eb
F
An - dy War - hol, won't you please come home?
G
C
C7
I been moth-ered, fa-thered, aunt and un - cled, Been
F
3
G
Roy Hal - eed and Art Gar - fun - kel'd. I just dis - cov - ered
C
some - bod - y's tapped my phone.

The 59th Street Bridge Song (Feelin' Groovy)

Eb Bb Cm7sus Bb Eb Bb Cm7 Bb
3
look - in' for fun and Feel - in' Groov - y.
Eb Bb Cm7sus Bb Eb Bb
Hel - lo lamp - post, what - cha know - in' I've come to watch your flow -
Cm7sus Bb Eb Bb Cm7sus Bb
- ers grow - in'. Ain't - cha got no rhymes for me?
Eb Bb Cm7sus Bb Eb Bb Cm7sus Bb
Doot - in' doo - doo, Feel - in' Groov - y. Got

Eb Bb Cm7sus Bb Eb Bb
no deeds to do, no prom-is-es to keep. I'm dap-pled and drow-sy and
Cm7 Bb Eb Bb Cm7 Bb
read-y to sleep. Let the morn-ing-time drop all its pet-als on me.
Eb Bb Cm7sus Bb Eb Bb Cm7sus Bb
Life, I love you, All is groov-y.
Eb Bb Cm7sus Bb Eb Bb Cm7sus Bb
Repeat and fade out

SIMON AND GARFUNKEL THEY AIN'T.

But they make the news. Often.

We report the news, dawn to dawn. We think it's the most important thing our listeners can get on the radio. We never leave it. We do nothing else.

Which means Washingtonians can get all the news. Like they've never heard it on the radio before.

If that news happens to include Simon and Garfunkel, fine.

But, in their own ways, De Gaulle and Kosygin are pretty mind-bending guys themselves.

WTOP RADIO
NONSTOP NEWS
A Post-Newsweek Station

The Dangling Conversation

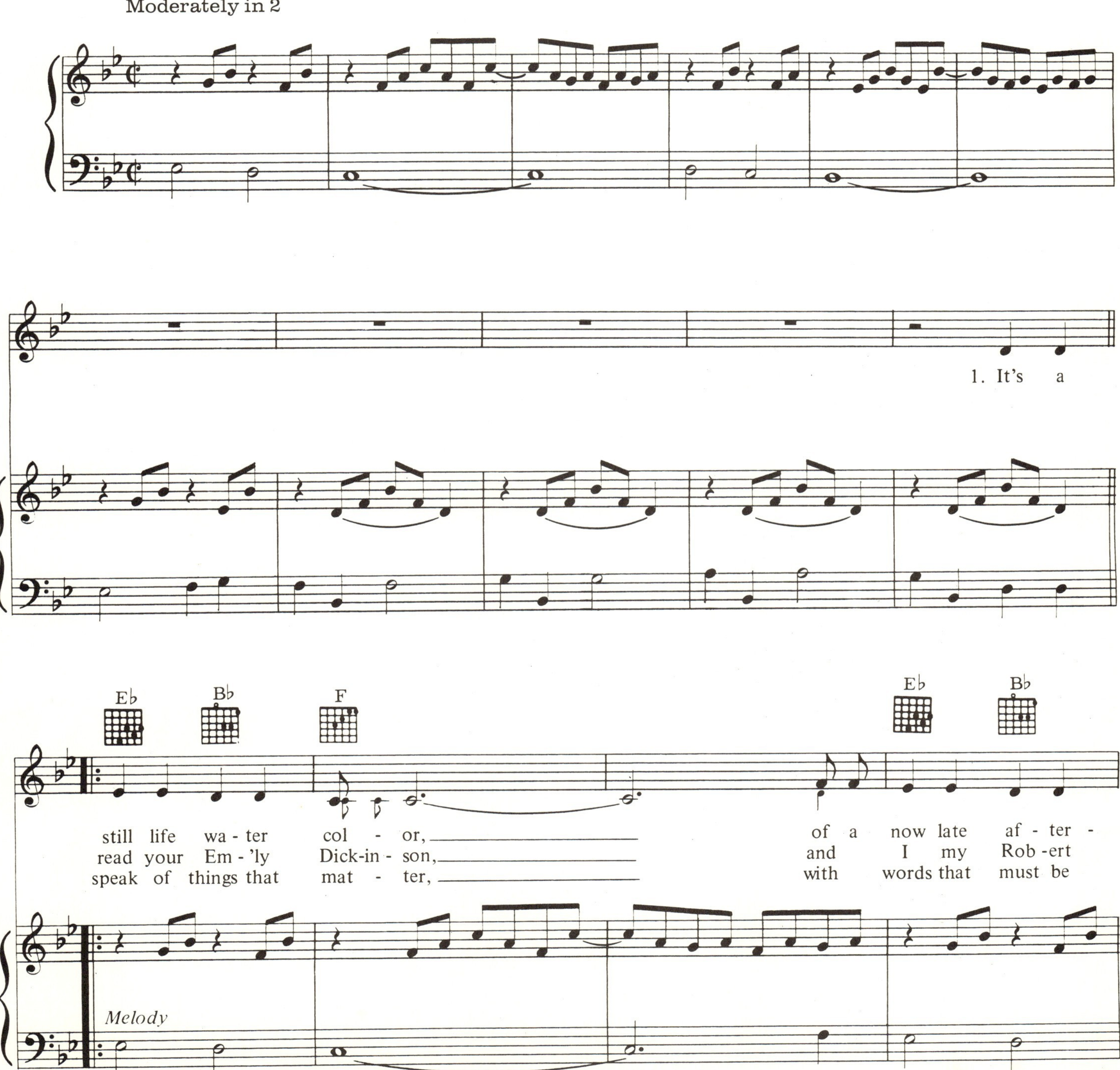

F
E♭
B♭
F
noon, As the sun shines through the cur-tained lace
Frost, And we note our place with book mark - ers
said, 'Can an - al - y - sis be worth-while?
B♭
B♭6
B♭maj7
and sha-dows wash the room.
that meas-ure what we've lost.
'Is the thea- ter real - ly dead?'
B♭6
Gm
And we sit and drink our cof - fee
Like a po - em poor - ly writ - ten we are
Now the room is soft - ly fad - ed and I
Melody
f
A♭
G
couched in our in - dif - fer - ence, like shells up - on the
vers - es out of rhy - thm, coup - lets out of
on - ly kiss your sha - dow, I can - not feel your

F
shore You can hear the o - cean roar in the
rhyme, in syn - co - pat - ed time and the
hand, you're a strang - er now un - to me lost in the
Melody
E♭
B♭
F
B♭
F
dang - ling con - ver - sa - tion and the sup - er - fi - cial
mp
E♭
B♭
sighs the borders of our lives.
are the
in the
B♭6
B♭maj7
1.2.
B♭6
3. B♭
2. And you
3. Yes, we
8va bassa

Flowers Never Bend With The Rainfall

C G Bm7 Cmaj7
I don't know what is real, I can't touch what I
I am blind-ed by the light of God and truth and
So my fan-ta-sy be-comes re-al-i-
G Bm Cmaj7 G C G
feel And I hide be-hind the shield of my il-lu-sion.
right And I wan-der in the night with-out di-rec-tion.
ty, And I must be what I must be and face to-mor-row.
Chorus:
D C G
So I'll con-tin-ue to con-tin-ue
Em C6
to pre-tend My life will nev-er

Em
A
C
end,
And Flow - ers
Nev - er Bend
G
1.2.
With
The Rain - fall.
2. The
3. No
3.
rall.
p
C9add11

For Emily, Whenever I May Find Her

C
F
rain.
I wan - dered emp - ty streets down
B♭
F
passed the shop dis - plays.
I heard ca -
E♭
B♭
the - dral bells
trip - ping down the al - ley ways,
as I
C
F
walked on.
And when you ran to me your
mf

B♭
F
cheeks flushed with the night. We walked on
E♭
frost - ed fields of ju - ni - per and lamp - light,
B♭
C
I held your hand.
F
B♭
And when I a - woke and felt you warm and near,

F
Eb
I kissed your hon - ey hair with my grate-ful
tears.
Bb
C
Oh I love you, girl.
Eb
Bb
Bbmaj9
Oh, I love
you.

A Poem On The Underground Wall

Am
E7
Am
F
Rest - less in an - tic - i - pa - tion, a man waits in the
Safe with - in his si - lent sock - et, he holds his col - ored
he hes - i - tates, then with - draws deep - er in the
1.2.
C
F
C
G
shad - ows.
cray - on.
Am
3.
C
Am
2. His
3. Now shad - ows.
Am
And the train is gone

C
sud - den - ly on wheels click - ing
F
Em
si - lent - ly like a gen - tly tap - ping lit - a -
Dm
Am
ny, And he holds his cray - on ro - sa - ry
F
C
Am
tight - er in his hand. Now

F C Dm C Am E7 Am
from his pock - et quick he flash - es, the cray - on on the wall he slash - es,
heart is laugh - ing, scream - ing, pound - ing, The poem a - cross the tracks re - bound - ing,
F C Dm C Am E7 Am
Deep up - on the ad - ver - tis - ing, a sin - gle word - ed poem com - prised of
Shad - owed by the ex - it light his legs take their as - cend - ing flight to
1.
F C
four let - ters
And his
2.
F C Am E7 Am
seek the breast of dark - ness and be suck - led by the night.
poco rit.

7 o'clock News/Silent Night

Db
Ab
child! Ho - ly In - fant so ten - der and
Eb7
Ab
mild, Sleep in heav - en - ly peace,
Eb7
Sleep in heav - en - ly
1.
Ab
peace!
2.
peace!
rall.
p

Narration

(Spoken over musical background of "Silent Night")
"This is the early evening edition of the news.
The recent fight in the House of Representatives was over the open housing section of the Civil Rights Bill.
Brought traditional enemies together but it left the defenders of the measure without the votes of their strongest supporters.
President Johnson originally proposed an outright ban covering discrimination by everyone for every type of housing but it had no chance from the start and everyone in Congress knew it.
A compromise was painfully worked out in the House Judiciary Committee.
In Los Angeles today comedian Lenny Bruce died of what was believed to be an overdose of narcotics.
Bruce was 42 years old.
Dr. Martin Luther King says he does not intend to cancel plans for an open housing march Sunday into the Chicago suburb of Cicero.
Cook County Sheriff Richard Ogleby asked King to call off the march and the police in Cicero said they would ask the National Guard be called out if it is held.
King now in Atlanta, Georgia plans to return to Chicago Tuesday.
In Chicago Richard Speck, accused murderer of nine student nurses, was brought before a Grand Jury today for indictment.
The nurses were found stabbed and strangled in their Chicago apartment.
In Washington the atmosphere was tense today as a special sub-committee of the House Committee on Un-American activities continued its probe into anti-Viet Nam war protests.
Demonstrators were forcibly evicted from the hearings when they began chanting anti-war slogans.
Former Vice President Richard Nixon says that unless there is a substantial increase in the present war effort in Viet Nam, the U.S. should look forward to five more years of war.
In a speech before the Convention of the Veterans of Foreign Wars in New York, Nixon also said opposition to the war in this country is the greatest single weapon working against the U.S.
That's the 7 o'clock edition of the news.
Goodnight."

BOOKENDS

Mrs. Robinson

B♭
Gm
B♭
God bless you, please, Mrs. Rob - in - son, Heav-en holds a place
Gm
E♭
Cm
for those who pray, (Hey, hey, hey,
G
hey, hey, hey.)
Verse:
G7
1. We'd like to know a lit - tle bit a - bout you for our files,

C7
We'd like to help you learn to help your-
C9
F7
B♭
self.
Look a-round you, all you see are
E♭
Cm
G
sym-pa-thet-ic eyes,
Stroll a-round
F7
the grounds un-til you feel at home.
And here's to you

D.S. al Coda

Coda
G
Verse:
G7
2. Hide it in a hid - ing place where no one ev - er goes,
3. Sit - ting on a so - fa on a Sun - day af - ter - noon,
C7
Put it in your pan - try with your cup - cakes,
Go - ing to the can - di - dates' de - bate,
F7
B♭
It's a lit - tle se - cret, just the Rob -
Laugh a - bout it, shout a - bout it,

E♭
Cm
G
- in - son's af - fair,
When you've got to choose,
Most of all,
Ev - 'ry way you look
F7
you've got to hide it from the kids.
at it, you lose.
Coo, coo, ca - choo,
Where have you gone,
Chorus:
B♭
Gm
B♭
Mrs. Rob - in - son,
Joe Di - mag - gi - o?
Je - sus loves you more
A na - tion turns its
Gm
E♭
F7
than you will know,
lone - ly eyes to you,
(Wo, wo, wo.)
(Woo, woo, woo.)

B♭
Gm
God bless you, please, Mrs. Rob - in - son,
What's that you say, Mrs. Rob - in - son,
B♭
Gm
E♭
Heav - en holds a place for those who pray.
"Jolt - in' Joe" has left and gone a - way.
Cm
G
(Hey, hey, hey, hey, hey, hey.
(Hey, hey, hey, hey, hey, hey.
1.
2. G7add6
)
)

Save The Life Of My Child

Dm7
Save The Life Of My Child, Cried the des - per - ate
C
F
moth - er. Ah, ah, ah,
C
G7
G
ah. A
wom - an from the sup - er - mark - et ran to call the cops. He

C
G
must be high on some - thing, some - one said. Though it
C
G
nev - er made the New York Times, In the Dail - y News the cap - tion
C
read Save The Life Of My
Dm7
C
Child, Cried the des - per - ate moth - er.

F
C
G7
Ah, ah, ah, ah.
G
A pa - trol car pass - ing by halt - ed to a stop. Said
C
G
of - fi - cer Mc - Dou - gal in dis - may, "The
G
C
G
G(sus)
force can't do a de - cent job 'Cause the kids got no re - spect for the law to -

Dm7
day." Save The Life Of My Child
C
Cried the des-per-ate moth-er. What's be-com-ing of the
F
C
chil-dren? Peo-ple ask-ing each oth-er.
G
When dark-ness fell, ex-cite-ment kissed the

C
crowd and made them wild, The at - mos - phere was freak - y hol - i -
G
day. When the spot - light hit the boy and the
G
C
crowd be - gan to cheer, He flew a - way!
F
C
C7
Oh, my grace, I've got no hid - ing place.
Repeat and fade out.

America

Bright waltz tempo
mf
Eb
Ebmaj7
Cm
Eb
Ab
"Let us be lov - ers, We'll mar - ry our for - tunes to - geth - er.
mp
Eb
Ebmaj7
I've got some real es - tate
Cm
Gm7
Here in my bag."
So we

Gm7
C7
Gm7
bought a pack of cig - a - rettes, And Mrs. Wag - ner's
C9
Gm7
F
E♭
B♭
pies, And walked off to look for A -
E♭
E♭maj7
Cm
Cm7
A♭
mer - i - ca.
E♭
E♭maj7
"Kath - y," I said, As we

Cm
Eb
Ab
board - ed a Grey - hound in Pitts - burgh,
Eb
Ebmaj7
"Mich - i - gan seems like a dream to me now.
Cm7
Bb
It took me four days To hitch - hike from
F
Bb
F
Ebmaj7
Sag - i - naw. I've come to look for A - mer -

E♭
D♭maj7
i - ca." Laugh - ing on the
D♭
E♭
bus, Play-ing games with the fac - es,
D♭maj7
She said the man in the gab - ar-dine
E♭
suit Was a spy.

Ab
Abmaj7
Eb
I said, "Be care - ful, His bow - tie is real - ly a cam - 'ra."
Ebmaj7
Cm7
Eb6
Cm6(sus)
E
Abmaj7
Eb
Ebmaj7
Cm
"Toss me a cig - a - rette, I think there's
Eb
Ab
one in my rain - coat."

E♭
E♭maj7
Cm
"We smoked the last one An hour — a - go." —
Gm7
Gm7
C9
So I looked at the scen - er - y, —
She read her mag - a - zine; — And the
F
E♭
B♭
E♭
E♭maj7
moon rose o - ver an o - pen

Cm7
Eb
Ab
field.
Eb
Ebmaj7
Cm
Eb
"Kath - y, I'm lost I said, Though I knew she was
Ab
Abmaj7
Fm7
Ab
Eb
sleep - ing.
I'm emp - ty and
Ebmaj7
Cm
ach - ing and I don't know why."

B♭
F
Counting the cars On the New Jersey Turnpike. They've all
B♭
F
E♭maj7
come to look for Amer - i -
E♭
F
B♭
ca, All come to
Repeat and fade.
F
E♭maj7
E♭
look for Amer - i - ca.

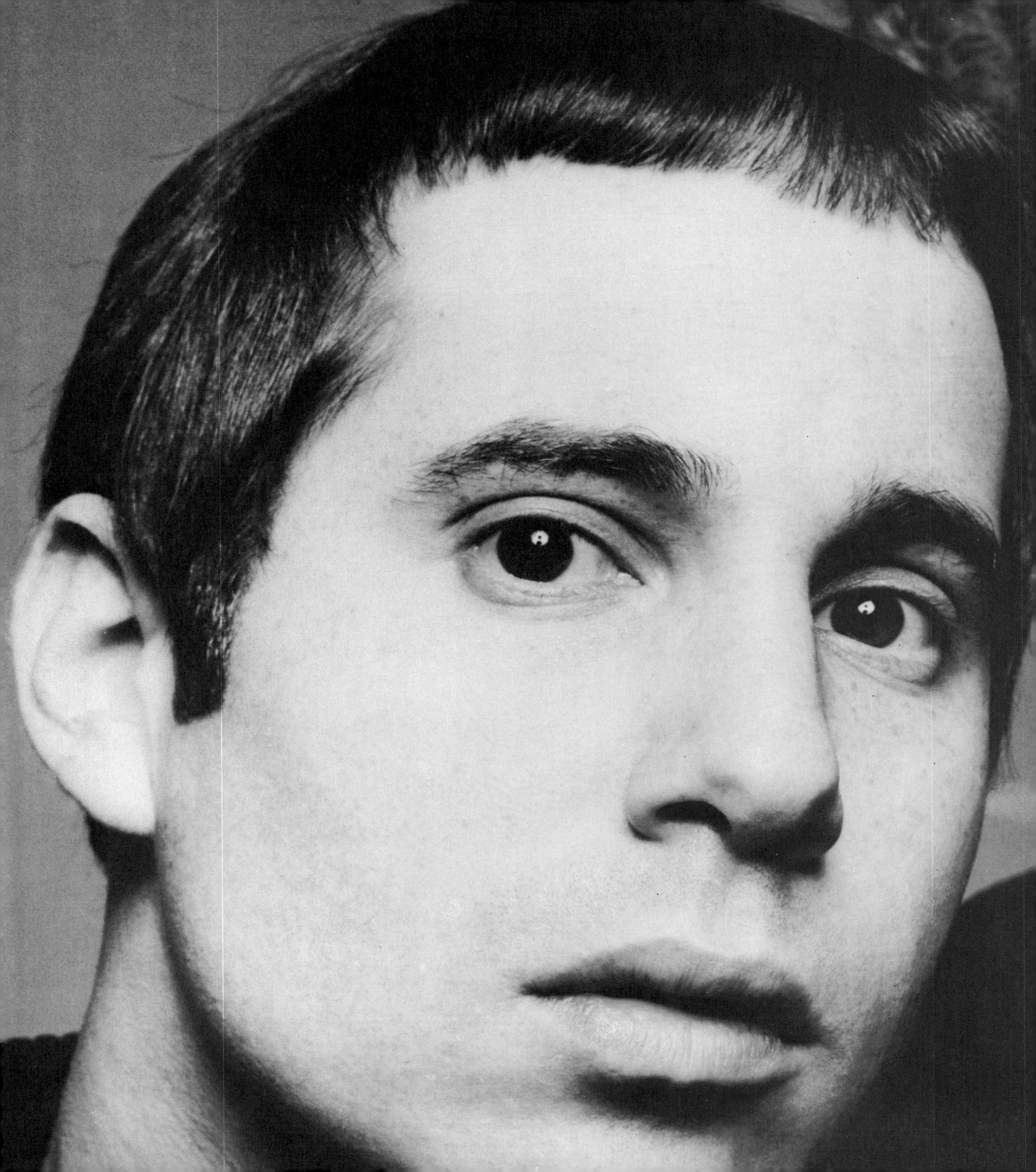

Overs

Rubato
D♯dim
Em
Why don't we stop fool - in' our - selves?
D
Em
The game is o - ver, o - ver, o - ver. No
Tempo
G
Gm6
D
F♯m
Bm
D
G
D
D6
good times, no bad times There's no times at all Just the

G E D Em(sus) G
New York Times Sit-tin' by the win-dow sill near the
D Gm Dmaj7 F♯dim
flow-ers. We might as well be a-
Em7 Dmaj7 G D
part It hard-ly mat-ters, we sleep sep-'rate-ly
Em F♯7 G Dmaj7 D6
And drop a smile pass-in' in the hall But there's

G
F♯m Dmaj7 Bm
Em7
E7
D
no laughs left 'Cause we laughed them all
And we laughed them
Em7
G6
all in a ver - y short time.
Time is tap - ping on my
F♯m
D
D6
E9
Em7(sus)
D
fore - head
Hang - ing from my mir - ror
E9
Em7(sus)
F♯m
Em
Gm6
Rat - tl - ing the tea cups
And I won - der

D F♯dim Em7 Gm6 D
how long? Can I de - lay We're just a hab - it like
G D Em7 F♯7 G C9
sac - cha - rine And I'm ha - bit - u - al - ly
D Dmaj7 D6 G F♯m Dmaj7 Bm
feel - in' kind - a blue But each time I try on the
E9
(Tacet)
thought of leav - in' you I stop! I stop and think it o - ver.

Old Friends

Slowly
A♭maj7 E♭maj7
Old Friends,
mf
mp
A♭maj7 E♭maj7 Fm7 B♭7 E♭ Cm
Old Friends, Sat on their park bench Like book - ends. A
Fm7 B♭ Cm
news - pap - er blown through the grass Falls on the round toes Of the
E♭maj7 A♭ E♭6 A♭maj7 E♭maj7 A♭maj7 E♭maj7
high shoes Of the Old Friends. Old Friends,

Fm7 Bb7 Abmaj7 Gm7 Fm7 Bb7
Win - ter com - pan - ions, The old men Lost in their o - ver - coats,
Eb Fm7 Cm Fm7 Bb7
Wait - ing for the sun - set. The sounds of the cit - y,
Gm7 Cm Bb
Sift - ing through trees, set - tle like dust On the
Ab Eb6 Fm7 Bb7
shoul - ders Of the Old Friends. Can you im - a - gine us

Ebmaj7
Ab
Abm
Eb
Years from to-day, Shar - ing a park bench qui - et - ly? How
Fm7
Bb7
Cm
Abmaj7
Ebmaj7
ter - ri - bly strange To be sev - en - ty. Old Friends,
Fm7
Bb7
Abmaj7
Gm7
Fm7
Bb7
mem - o - ry brush - es the same years. Si - lent - ly shar - ing the
Eb6
Cm
Abmaj7
Ebmaj7
Abmaj7
Ebmaj7
same fears.
poco ritard

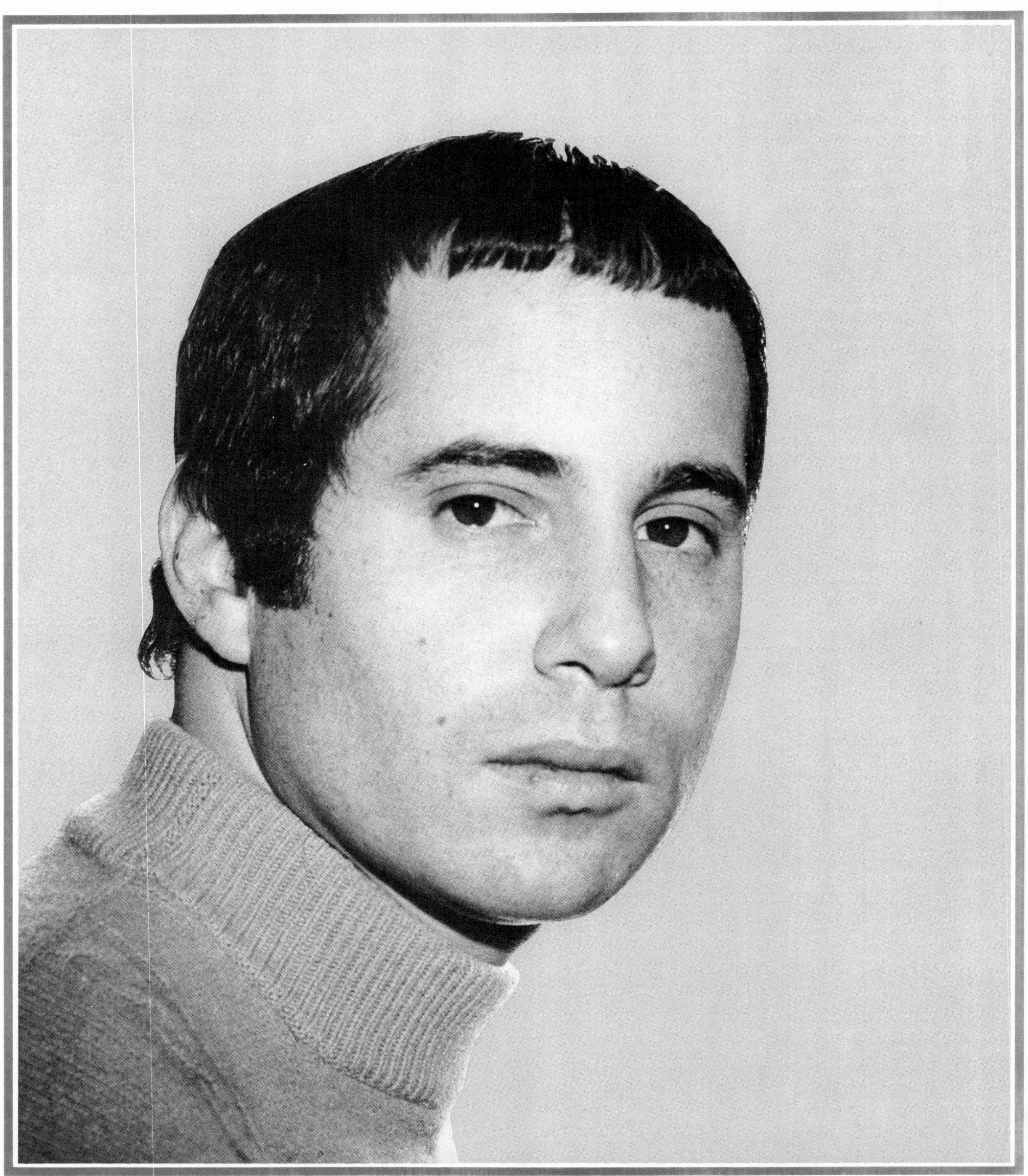

Bookends

Gracefully
Fm7
Time it was, And what a
time it was, it was
Eb
A time of
Fm7
in - no - cence, A time of
Eb
con - fi - den - ces.

Fm7
Long a - go it must be I have a
Eb
Fm7
pho - to - graph Pre - serve your mem - o - ries; They're all that's
Eb
Fm7
left you.
Eb
Fm7
Eb
ritard

Fakin' It

Moderate tempo, with a beat
Eb
Eb7
When she goes she's gone,
mf
mp
Ab
Gm
Ab
G
C
If she stays she stays here.
The
F
C
Bb9
Ab
Gm
Fm
girl does what she wants to do, She knows what she wants to do and I know I'm
3

E♭
A♭
Gm
Fm
E♭
E♭7
Fak-in' it,
I'm not real - ly mak-in' it.
E♭
E♭7
I'm such a dub - i - ous soul
A♭
Gm
A♭
G
C
Dm7
C
and a walk in the gar - den wears me down.
F
C
F
Tang - led in the fall - en vines,
Pick - in' up the punch lines,

A♭maj7
Gm
Fm7
E♭
A♭
A♭maj7
Gm7
Fm7
I've just been Fak - in' it, Not real - ly
E♭
E♭7
mak - in' it.
(Spoken): No, no, no, no.
E♭
E♭7
A♭
Gm7
Is there an - y dan - ger?
No, no, not
A♭
G
C
real - ly, Just lean on me.

F
C6
Fmaj7
F
Take the time to treat your friend-ly neigh-bors hon-est-ly,
Ab
Gm
Fm
Eb
Fm
Eb
Ab
Gm
Fm
I've just been Fak-in' it, Fak-in' it, Not real-ly
Eb
Ab
Gm
Fm
Eb
Fm
Eb
mak-in' it; This feel-in' of Fak-in' it,
Ab
Gm
Fm
Eb
Eb7
I still have-n't shak-en it.

E♭
E♭7
A♭
Gm
A♭
G7
Pri - or to this life - time I sure - ly was a tail - or. Look at
p
3
C
G7
me.
3
3
C
F
C
(Spoken): Good morning, Mr. Leach, have you had a busy day?
I own a tail - or's face and hands,
3
F7
A♭
I am the tail - or's face and hands.

A♭ A♭maj7 Gm7 Fm7 E♭ A♭ Gm7 Fm7
I know I'm Fak-in' it, Fak-in' it, I'm not real-ly
E♭ A♭ Gm7 Fm E♭ A♭ Gm Fm
mak-in' it, This feel-in' of Fak-in' it I still have-n't
E♭ A♭ E♭
shak-en it, shak-en it. I know I'm Fak-in' it,
A♭ Gm Fm E♭ A♭ E♭
I'm not real-ly mak-in' it.
Repeat and fade

Punky's Dilemma

Am
sion - al - ly plays L. A.
than an - y or - din-ar - y jam. I'm a
Fmaj7
Gm7
Fmaj7
1.
Cas - u - al - ly glanc - ing at his toup - ee.
cit - i - zens for boy-sen-ber-ry jam fan.
2.
B♭maj7
Ah, South Cal - i -
Fmaj7
Gm7
forn - ia. If I be-come a First Lieu-ten - ant

C7
Fmaj7
Gm
would you put my pho — to on your pia-no?
To Mar-y Jane
Fmaj7
B♭
Best wish-es Mar-tin.
Old Rod-ger, draft dod-ger
Am
Fmaj7
B♭
leav-in' by the base-ment door.
Ev-'ry-bod-y knows what he's
B♭maj7
B♭6
Fmaj7
Gm7
tip-py toe-ing down there for.
Repeat and fade.

A Hazy Shade Of Winter

C
Dm
C
hard to please, But look a-round, leaves are brown And the sky
B♭
A7
Dm
is A Ha-zy Shade Of Win-ter. Hear the Sal-va-tion
C
B♭
Ar-my Band, Down by the riv-er-side, It's bound to be a bet-ter ride, than
Am
C
what you've got planned, Car-ry your cup in your hand, And look a-round,

Dm
C
B♭7
A7
leaves are brown now, And the sky is a Ha - zy Shade Of Win -
Dm
C
- ter. Hang on - to your hopes, my friend,
B♭
Am
3
That's an eas - y thing to say, but if your hopes should pass a - way, Simp - ly pre - tend that you can
C
Dm
C7
build them a - gain. Look a - round; The grass is high, the fields are

B♭7
A7
Dm
ripe: It's the spring - time of my life.
B♭
F
Fmaj7
Sea - sons change with the scen - er - y, Weav - ing time in a
C9
Dm
A7
Dm
tap - es - try. Won't you stop and re - mem - ber me,
C
B♭
At an - y con - ven - ient time?
Fun - ny how my mem - 'ry skips, while

Am
C
look-in' o-ver man-u-scripts of un-pub-lished rhyme, Drink-ing my vod-ka and lime.
Dm
C7
B♭7
I look a-round Leaves are brown now, And the sky is A Ha-
A7
Dm
C
B♭7
-zy Shade Of Win-ter. Look a-round; Leaves are brown, There's a patch
1. A7
Dm
2. A7
Dm
of snow on the ground. Look a-round; of snow on the ground.

At The Zoo

Moderate tempo
Cmaj7
C7
Some-one told me, it's all hap-pen-ing At The Zoo.
mp
F
F7
Bb
F
C7
I do be-lieve it, I do be-lieve it's true.
Bb
F7
Bb
D7
Gm
D7
(Hum)
(Hum)

Gm
B♭
F7
B♭
D7
Gm
D7
(Hum)
(Hum)
Gm
Dm7
B♭
Gm
Dm7
B♭
Dm7
It's a light and tum-ble jour - ney, from the East - side to the park
mf
Gm
Dm7
B♭
Dm
Gm
Dm7
F
F7
Just a fine and fan-cy ram-ble to the zoo.
B♭
D7
Gm7
Dm7
B♭
D7
Gm
Dm7
But you can take the cross - town bus, if it's rain - in' or it's cold, And the

Bb
D7
Gm
Dm7
C6
an - i - mals will love it, if you do, if you
Gm
C6
Gm
do. Oo Oo
Cmaj7
C7
mp
Some-thing tells me, it's all hap - pen - ing At The Zoo.
F
F7
Bb
F
Gm
I do be - lieve it, I do be - lieve it's true.

Dm7
B♭
F7
B♭
D7
Gm
D7
Gm
(Hum)
(Hum)
Oh
B♭
F7
B♭
D7
Gm
D7
Gm
F7
B♭
D7
(Hum)
The mon - keys stand for
mf
Gm
Dm7
B♭
D7
Gm 11
Gm
Dm7
B♭
D7
hon - es - ty, Gir - affes are in - sin - cere, And the el - e - phants are
Gm
Dm7
F
F7
B♭
D7
Gm
Dm7
kind - ly, but they're dumb. O - rang - u - tans are skep - ti - cal of

B♭ D7 Gm Dm7 B♭ D7 Gm Dm7
chan - ges in their ca - ges, And the zoo - keep - er is ve - ry fond — of
B♭ Gm Dm7 B♭ D7 Gm Dm7 B♭ D7
rum. — Ze - bras are re - ac - tion - a - ries, An - te - lopes are
Gm Dm7 B♭ D7 Gm Dm7 B♭ D7
mis - sion - a - ries, Pig - eons plot in se - cre - cy, — And ham - sters turn on
Gm B♭ Gm B♭ D7 Gm
fre - quent - ly — What a gas! — You got - ta come and see — At The Zoo. — At The
Repeat and fade

BRIDGE OVER TROUBLED WATER

Cecilia

Moderate, not too fast, rhythmically

B♭
F
1. C
2. C
beg-ging you please to come home.
Ho - ho - home.
mp
F
B♭
Mak-ing love in the af - ter - noon with Ce - ci -
F
B♭
F
C
F
(mak - ing love)
- lia, Up in my bed - room,
I got up to wash
B♭
F
C
F
my face When I come back to bed, some-one's tak - en my place.

F
B♭
F
B♭
F
Cel - ia, You're break-ing my heart, You're shak-ing my con - fi - dence dai -
mf
C
B♭
F
B♭
F
- ly. Oh, Ce - cil - ia, I'm down on my knees, I'm
B♭
F
C
F
beg-ging you please to come home. Come on home. Poh poh
mp
mf
Fsus
F
B♭
C
poh poh poh poh poh poh poh poh poh poh poh. Ju - bi -

B♭
F
la - tion, She loves me a - gain, I fall on the floor and I laugh-
f
mf
1.
C
- ing. Ju - bi -
2.
ing. Oh oh oh oh oh
oh oh oh oh oh oh oh oh oh oh oh oh oh. Oh oh
rall.
oh. Come on home.

Keep The Customer Satisfied

E♭ B♭ E♭
slan - dered, Li - beled, I hear words I nev - er heard In the Bi -
A♭ E♭ Cm E♭
- ble. And I'm one step a-head of the shoe shine, Two steps a-way from the
Cm A♭ E♭ E♭7 A♭ 1. E♭
coun-ty line, Just trying to keep my cus-tom-ers sat - is - fied, Sat - is - fied.
2. E♭
fied. Woh Woh
f
A♭ (A♭ bass) E♭
Woh Woh

Eb
Ab
Eb
But it's the same old sto - ry
Ab
Eb
Bb
Eb
Ev - 'ry-where I go, I get slan-dered, Li - beled, I hear words
Ab
Eb
I nev - er heard In the Bi - ble. And I'm so
Cm
Eb
Cm
Bb
tired, I'm oh so tired, But I'm
Eb
Eb7
Ab
Eb
Ab7
trying to keep my cus-tom-ers sat - is - fied, Sat - is - fied.

So Long, Frank Lloyd Wright

F
Gm
E♭maj7
So soon
So soon.
Em7-5
D
I'll re - mem - ber
D7
B♭7
C
F6noC
Frank Lloyd Wright.
A7
Dm
Dm7
F7
B♭maj7
All of the nights we'd har - mo - nize till dawn.

B♭
F
I nev - er laughed so long
So long
Gm
G♭
G♭maj7
F
So long.
F7
Gm7
Fmaj7
Ar - chi-tects may come and Ar - chi-tects may go and nev -
E♭9
F
Gm7
Fm7
- er change your point of view.
When I
mf
dim. poco - - -

E♭7 E♭7-5 D7-5 Gmaj7 G7 C♯dim G7
run dry I stop a - while and think of you.
a - - poco
Gm7 Fmaj7
Ar - chi - tects may come and Ar - chi - tects may go and nev -
mp
E♭9 F Dmaj7
- er change your point of view. So
D7 B♭7 C F6noC
Long, Frank Lloyd Wright,
mp mf mp

A7
Dm
Dm7
F7
B♭maj7
All of the nights we'd har - mo - nize till dawn.
f
B♭
F
I nev - er laughed so long
So long
mf
mp
Keep repeating and fade out
G
G♭
F
G♭add A
So long
So long
dim. poco a poco
G
G♭
G♭maj7
F
G♭add A
So long.
So long

The Boxer

Moderate tempo
C
Am
G
C
I am just a poor boy. Though my
sto - ry's sel - dom told, I have squan-dered my re - sis - tance for a
pock - et - ful of mum - bles, such are prom - is - es.
mf
mp

Am
G
F
All lies and jest, still a man hears what he wants to hear, And
C
G
dis - re - gards the rest.
C
When I left my home and my fam - i - ly, I was

Am
G
no more than a boy in the com - pa - ny of stran - gers in the
Dm7
C
qui - et of a rail - way sta - tion run - ning scared,
Am
C
F
Lay - ing low, seek - ing out the poor - er quar - ters where the
G
F
Em
Dm
rag - ged peo - ple go, Look-ing for the plac - es on - ly they would

C
Am
know.
Lie - la - lie,
Lie - la -
G
Am
G
lie la lie - la - lie lie - la - lie
Lie - la -
F
G
C
lie la la la la Lie - la la la la lie.
Ask - ing on - ly work - man's wag - es I come

Am
G
look - ing for a job, but I get no of - fers,
Just a
Dm7
C
come-on from the whores on Sev-enth Av - e - nue.
Am
Dm7
G
F
I do de - clare, there were times when I was so lone-some I
C
G
took some com - fort there. Ooo - la - la la - la la la.

C
C
Then I'm lay - ing out my
G7
C
Am
G
win - ter clothes and wish - ing I was gone, go - ing home
Dm7
G7
G
C
Where the New York Cit - y win - ters are - n't bleed - ing me,
Em
Am
Lead - ing me,

G
C
go - ing home.
C
In the clear - ing stands a box - er, and a fight - er by his
Am
G
G7
trade, And he car - ries the re - mind - ers of ev - 'ry glove that
C
Dm7
G7
C
laid him down Or cut him till he cried out in his an - ger and his shame,

Am
G
F
C
"I am leav - ing, I am leav - ing." But the fight - er still re-mains.
G
C
G
F
C
Lie - la
Fade
Am
G
Am
lie, Lie - la - lie la lie -la - lie Lie - la - lie
G
F
C
Lie - la lie la la la la lie - la la la la lie. Lie - la

Baby Driver

Moderate bright tempo

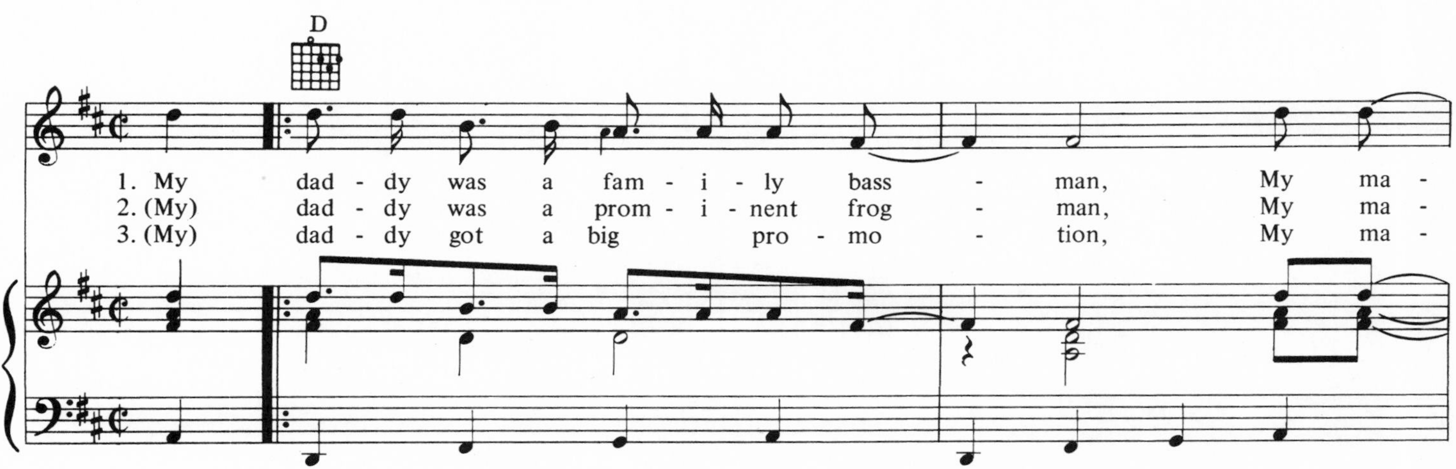

G
gray morn With music comin' in my ears
ried a gun But I never got the chance to serve
alone Oh, come into my room and play
D
In my ears. They call
I did not serve. They call
Yes, we can play. I'm not talk-
G
me Baby Driver, And once upon a pair of wheels
me Baby Driver, And once upon a pair of wheels
in' about your pigtails, But talkin' 'bout your sex appeal
D
Hit the road and I'm gone ah
Hit the road and I'm gone ah
Hit the road and I'm gone ah
D D♭ Am B7
What's my number, I
What's my number, I
What's my number, I
3

Em
Em7
won - der how your en - gine feels. Ba Ba Ba Ba
won - der how your en - gine feels. Ba Ba Ba Ba
won - der how your en - gine feels. Ba Ba Ba Ba
D
Db
Am
B7
Scoot down the road, What's my num - ber, I
Scoot down the road, What's my num - ber, I
Scoot down the road, What's my num - ber, I
Em7
D
won - der how your en - gine feels.
won - der how your en - gine feels.
won - der how your en - gine feels.
1, 2.
3.
2. My
3. My
Repeat and fade

The Only Living Boy In New York

C
F
Am7
Dm7
F
Fly down to Mex - i - co.
G
F
Da - n - da - da - n - da - da - n - da - da and here I am, The
mf
mp
C
F
C
On - ly Liv-ing Boy In New York.
r.h.
F
C
Dm7
C
F
I get the news I need from the weath-er re - port.
r.h.

C
I can gath-er all the news I need from the weath-er re-port.
F
C
Hey, I've got noth-ing to
3
r.h.
mf
F C Dm F6 G
do to-day but smile. Da-n-da-da-n-do-da-n-do-n
F
C
here I am, The On-ly Liv-ing Boy In New
mp

F
Am
York.
r.h.
mf
Dm
G7
C
Half of the time we're gone but we don't know where, And we don't know
f
dim. poco a poco
where.
Tom, get your plane right on
mp
time.
I know that you've been ea - ger to fly

F
C
now.
Hey
let your hon - es - ty
mf
F
C
Dm
F
G
shine, shine, shine now, Do - da - n - do - da - n - do -
da - n - do like it shines on me. The
Fmaj7
F6
F
mp
C
F
On - ly Liv - ing Boy In New York. The

C
F
C
On - ly Liv-ing Boy In New York.
p r.h.
rall.
pp

Why Don't You Write Me?

Moderate, with a strong beat

Cm
Gm
-ing so hard to be near you.
Eb
Ab
Eb
(Falsetto:) La la la.
(Basso) Why don't you write? Some-thing is wrong
(Sing:)
p
mp
F7
and I know I got to be there.
(yeah)
Bb7
May-be I'm lost, but I can't make the cost of the air-

Cm
Gm
E♭
A♭
fare. (oo) Tell me why
Why
mf
Tell me why
Why
B♭
Why
Why
E♭
Why Don't You Write Me? A let - ter would bright - en my lone -
mp
F7
B♭7
- li - est eve - ning. Mail it to - day if it's on -

Cm
Gm
-ly to say___ that you're leav - ing me.___
(Oo)___
Eb
Ab
Eb
Eb7
(Falsetto:) La la___ la.
p
mp
Ab7
(Sing:) Mon-day morn-ing, sit-ting in the sun Hop - ing and wish-ing for the mail___ to come.
mf
Eb
Eb7
Ab7
Tues-day, nev-er got a word, mmm.___
Wednes-day, Thurs-day, ain't no sign, Drank_
mp
mf

Eb
a half a bot - tle of i - o - dine. Fri - day, woe is me, I'm
Eb7
Ab
gon - na hang my bod - y from the high - est tree. (Falsetto:) Why Don't You Write
gliss.
mf
Eb
Ab
Me? (Sing:) Why Don't You Write Me?
dim. poco a poco
Ab7
Eb
Why Don't You Write Me? Why Don't You Write

Song For The Asking

E♭ B♭ E♭ F7 B♭
wait - ing all my life.
Gm Dm D Bdim Cm F7
Think-ing it o-ver, I've been sad,
Think-ing it o-ver, I'd be more than glad To
5
B♭ B♭7 G E♭ Gm Cm7
change my ways for the ask - ing,
Ask me and I will
D D7 E♭ B♭ E♭ B♭ F7 B♭
play All the love that I hold in - side.

El Condor Pasa (If I Could)

G
C
G
swan that's here and gone. A man gets tied up to the ground, He gives the world its sad-dest
Em
sound, its sad-dest sound.
I'd rath-er be a for-est than a
G
Em
street. Yes I would. If I could, I sure-ly would.
I'd rath-er feel the earth be-neath my
G
Em
C
feet. Yes I would. If I on-ly could, I sure-ly would.
3
3
G
C

G
Em

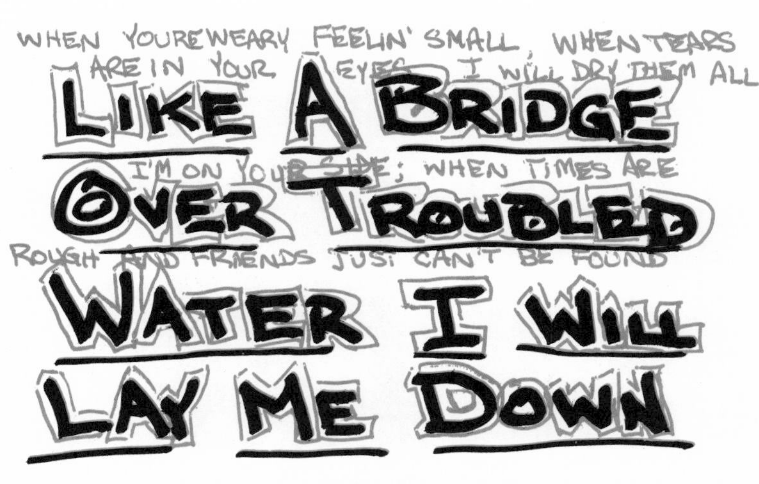

WHEN YOUREWEARY FEELIN' SMALL, WHEN TEARS
ARE IN YOUR EYES I WILL DRY THEM ALL
LIKE A BRIDGE
I'M ON YOUR SIDE; WHEN TIMES ARE
OVER TROUBLED
ROUGH AND FRIENDS JUST CAN'T BE FOUND
WATER I WILL
LAY ME DOWN
GOD I WILL
DOWN AND OUT
WHEN YOU'RE WEARY, ON THE STREET
LIKE A BRIDGE
WHEN EVENING FALLS SO HARD
OVER TROUBLED
I WILL BE THERE I'LL TAKE YOUR PART
WATER I WILL
WHEN DARKNESS FALLS AND PAIN IS ALL
EASE YOUR MIND
YOU FIND

Bridge Over Troubled Water

Eb Ab Eb Bb Cm Bb
I'm on your side. Oh,
I'll take your part. Oh,
Bb9 Eb Eb (D bass) In tempo Eb7 Eb9 Ab F
when times get rough And friends just can't be found,
when dark - ness comes And pain is all a - round,
Bb Eb7 Eb9 Ab F#dim (A bass) Eb (Bb bass) C7sus C7
Like a Bridge O - ver Trou-bled Wa - ter
Ab G7 Cm Eb7 Eb9 Ab F#dim (A bass) 1. Eb (Bb bass) C7sus C7
I will lay me down. Like a Bridge O - ver Trou-bled Wa-ter

Ab
Bb9 (sus)
Bb7
Eb
Ab
I will lay me down.
mf
f
Eb
Ab
Eb
Ab
Rubato
When you're
mf
mp
mf
mp
p
2
Eb (Bb bass)
Cm
Ab
Cm (G bass)
G
Cm
F7
Trou-bled Wa-ter I will lay me down.
mf
f
Eb
Ab
Cm
Ab
Abm
Eb

Ab
Eb
Ab
Eb
Ab
Sail on
Eb
Ab
Db
Ab
sil - ver girl,
Sail on by.
Your time has
Eb
Ab
Eb
Ab
Eb
Ab
come to shine.
All your dreams are on their way.
Eb
Bb
Cm
Bb
Eb
Eb (D bass)
See how they shine.
Oh,
if you need a friend
mp

In tempo
Eb7
Eb9
Ab
F
Bb
Eb7
Eb9
Ab
F#dim (A bass)
I'm sail-ing right be-hind.
Like a Bridge O-ver
Eb (Bb bass)
Cm
Ab
Cm
G
Cm
Eb7
Eb9
Ab
Abmaj7
F7 (A bass)
Trou-bled Wa-ter
I will ease your mind.
Like a Bridge O-ver
Eb (Bb bass)
Cm
Ab
G7
Cm
F9
Fmaj9
Trou-bled Wa-ter
I will ease your mind.
Eb (Bb bass)
Ab
Abm
Eb
rall.

—UPI Telephoto

PAUL SIMON

Mother And Child Reunion

Em
oh, lit - tle dar - ling of mine.
1. I can't for the
2. I just can't be -
D
life of me
lieve it's so,
re - mem - ber a sad - der day,
and though it seems strange to say,
Em
D
I know they say let it be,
I nev - er been laid so low
But it just don't work
in such a mys -
Em
C
out that way,
te - ri - ous way,
And the course of a life - time runs
And the course of a life - time runs

D
o - ver and o - ver a - gain. No, I
o - ver and o - ver a - gain. But I
C D G C D
would not give you false hope on this strange and mourn - ful
G C D G Em
day, When the Moth-er And Child Re - u - nion is
Am G D
on - ly a mo-tion a - way, Oh, oh the
3

C
D
G
C
D
Moth - er And Child Re - u - nion is on - ly a mo - tion a - way,
G
C
D
Oh, the Moth - er And Child Re -
G
Em
Am
G
D
u - nion is on - ly a mo- ment a - way.
G

Duncan

Moderately slow and steady
mp
Em
D
1. Couple in the next room bound to win a prize, They've been
mf
G
A
D
C
G
go - in' at it all night long, Well, I'm tryin' to get some sleep, but these
C
G
C
G
mo - tel walls are cheap, - Lin - coln Dun - can is my name and here's my

D
Em
song, here's my song.
Em
D
2. My fath - er was a fish - er - man, my ma - ma was a fish - er - man's friend, And
G
A
D
I was born in the bore - dom and the chow - der, So
C
G
C
G
when I reached my prime, I left my home in the Mar - i - times,

C
G
D
Em
Head - ed down the turn - pike for New Eng - land,__ sweet New Eng - land.
C
G
C
G
C
Instrumental solo
G
Em
D
Em
Em
D
3. Holes in my con - fi - dence,_ holes in the knees of my jeans, I's

G
A
D
C
G
left with - out a pen - ny in my pock - et,
Oo hoo hoo wee, I's a - bout
C
G
C
G
des - ti - tut - ed as a kid could be, And I wished I wore a ring so I could
D
Em
hock it, I'd like to hock it.
4. A
Em
D
5
young girl in a park - ing lot was preach - in' to a crowd, sing - in'
5

G
A
D
sa - cred songs and read - ing from the Bi - ble,
Well, I
C
G
C
G
told her I was lost,
and she told me all a - bout the Pen - te - cost,
And I
C
G
D
seen that girl as the road to my sur - vi - - - - -
Em
C
G
C
val.
Instrumental solo

G
C
G
Em
D
Em
Em
5. Just lat - er on the ver - y same night when I
D
G
A
crept to her tent with a flash - light, And my long years of in - no - cence
D
C
G
end - ed,
Well, she took me to the woods, say - in',

C
G
C
G
"Here comes some - thin' and it feels so good!" And just like a dog I was be -
D
Em
friend - ed, I was be - friend - ed.
Em
D
6. Oh, oh, what a night, oh, what a gar - den of de - light, Ev - en
G
A
D
now that sweet mem - o - ry ling - ers, I was

C
G
C
G
play - in' my gui - tar, ly - ing un - der - neath the stars, Just
C
G
D
Em
thank - in' the Lord for my fin - gers, for my fin - gers.
Fade out
C
G
C
G
C
G
Em
D
Em

Everything Put Together Falls Apart

Dm7
Cmaj7
Em7
Am
Em
D
(F♯ bass)
uh huh, I ain't blind, no, some folks are
Dm
(F bass)
Dm7
G7
C7
cra - zy, oth - ers walk that bor - der line, watch what you're do - in', Tak - in'
Fm7
Cadd9
F7
Cm7
(F bass)
downs to get off to sleep, and ups to start you on your
B♭
B
B♭
A
E
way; Af - ter a while they'll change your style,

E7 A Am Em F♯m E A E7
Mm I see it hap - pen - in ev - 'ry day.
Dm7 Cmaj7 Em7 Am E D (F ♯ bass)
Uh huh, spare your heart. ev - 'ry - thing
Dm (F bass) Dm7 G7 C7
put to - geth - er soon - er or lat - er falls a - part, there's noth - in'
Fm7
to it, noth - in' to it. You can cry and you can

C
F7
Cm7 (F bass)
lie, For all the good it - 'll do you, you can die,
Bb
B
Bb
A
Oh, but when it's done and the po - lice come, and they're lay -
E
E7
A
Am
- in' you down for dead, Uh huh, just re -
Em
F#m
E
E7
A
Am
Em
F#m7
E
mem - ber what I said!

Run That Body Down

G
C7
Am
E+
Ah,
F
G
G7
C
3
She said, "Paul, you bet - ter look a - round.
F
G7
C
C7
3
How long you think that you can Run That Bod - y Down?
F
G7
C
C7
F
E
How man - y nights you think that you can do what you been do - - -

Am
Dm7
G7
C
Am
Dm
E+
E
in'? Who___ now, who you fool - in'?"
Am
Dm
G
C
G
C7
I came back home and I__ went in - to bed.__
Am
E+
F
Am
Ah, ___ I was rest - in' my head.___
Dm
G
C
G
C7
My wife came in and she said, "What's wrong,_ sweet boy,___ what's wrong?"__

Am E+ F G G7
Ah, I told her what's wrong. I said,
C F G7
"Peg, you bet-ter look a-round. How long you think that you can
C C7 F G7 C C7
Run That Bod-y Down? How man-y nights you think that you can do what you been do-
F E Ar Dm G7 C Am
in'? Who now, who you fool-in'?"
Fade out

Armistice Day

D7
D
G
a - hoo.
F♯m
Em
D
Mm
3
G
D
5
4
4
4
No long drawn blown out ex - cus - es were made, When I
G
F♯m
Em
(Omit 3rd)
D
(Omit 3rd)
2
4
need - ed a friend, she was there,

A
(Omit 3rd)
D
Just like an eas - - - y chair.
D
G
Oo
Oo
F#m
Em
D
Mm
D
Ar - mis - tice Day,
Ar - mis - tice Day,

G
F♯m
Em
(Omit 3rd)
D
(Omit 3rd)
That's all I real - ly want - ed to say.
A
(Omit 3rd)
D
(Omit 3rd)
D
Oh, I'm wear - y from wait - ing in Wash - ing - ton D. C.
Oh, con-gress wo - man, won't you tell that con - gress man,
G
D
I'm com - ing to see my con - gress - man, but he's a
I've wait - ed such a long time, I've 'bout wait - ed

A
(D bass)
void - in' me.
all I can.
Wear - y from
Oh, con - gress
G
(D bass)
D
wait - ing down in Wash - ing - ton D. C.
wo - man, won't you tell that con - gress - man.
1.
2.
Fade

Me And Julio Down By The Schoolyard

No chord
D
It's a - gainst the law,
It was a - gainst the
G
law,
What the ma - ma saw,
D
It was a - gainst the law.
G
The
(In a)
G
ma - ma looked down and spit on the ground ev - 'ry time my name gets
cou - ple of days they come and take me a - way, but the press let the sto - ry

C
D
men - tioned,
leak,
The pa - pa said, "Oy, if I
And when the rad - i - cal priest come to
get that boy I'm gon - na stick him in the house of de - ten -
get me re - leased, we's all on the cov - er of News -
G
No chord
C
- tion."
- week.
Well, I'm on my way,
G
C
I don't know where I'm go - in',
I'm on my way,

G A D
I'm tak - in' my time___ but I don't know where.___ Good - bye
C F G
Ro - - - sie, the Queen of Co - ro - na,
F C (E bass) D
See you, Me And Ju - lio Down By The School - yard.___
G C G D G F
___ See you, Me And Ju - lio

C
(E bass)
D
1. G
C
G
D
Down By The School - yard.
In a
2. G
C
G
D
G
F
See you, Me And Ju - lio
C
(E bass)
D
G
C
G
D
Down By The School - yard.
Fade out
G
C
G
D
Instrumental solo

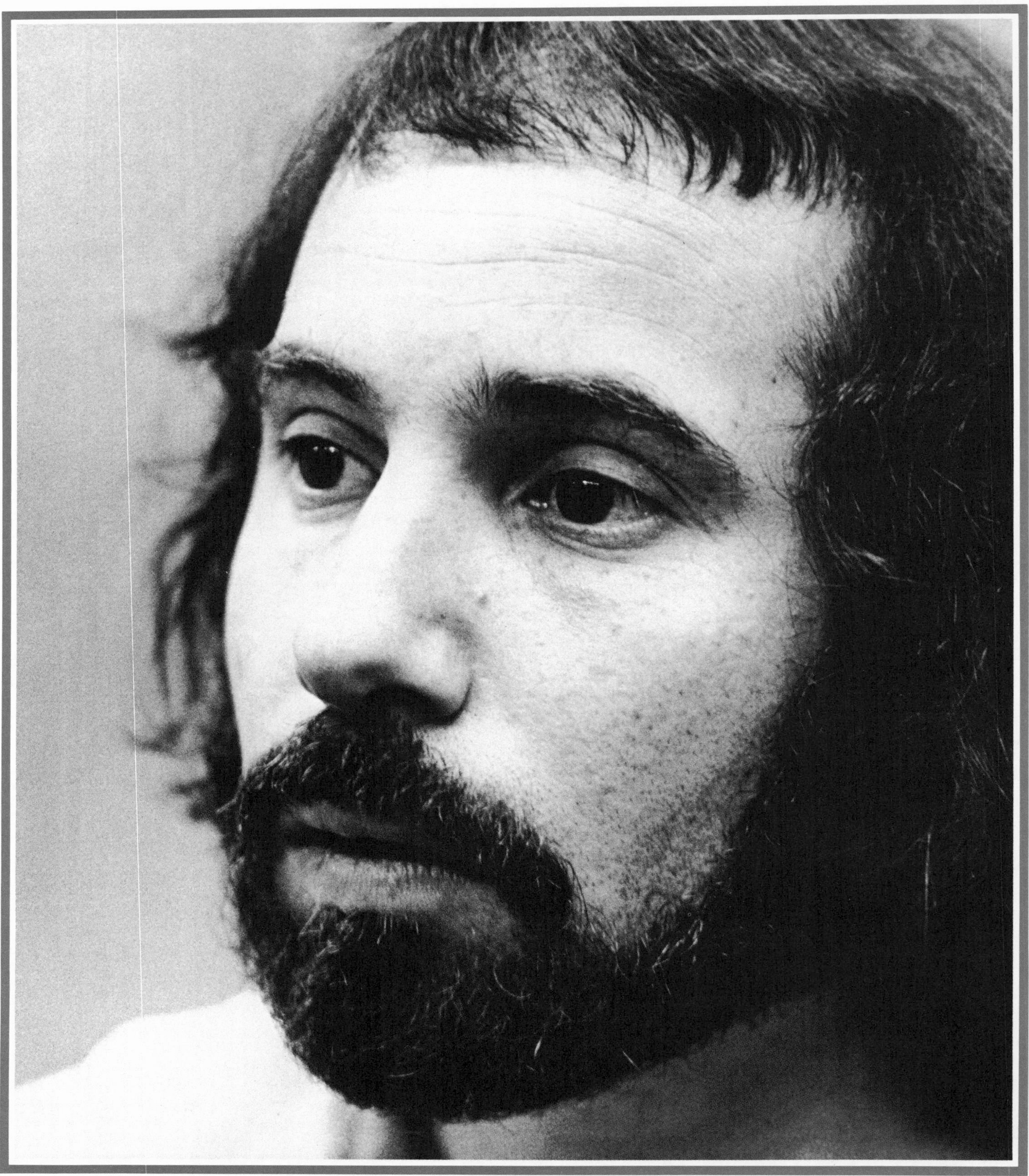

Peace Like A River

Dm
oh, we were sat - is - fied.
Dm
Oh, when I re - mem - ber
Gm
F
B♭
F
mis - in - for - ma - tion fol - lowed us like a plague,
B♭
F
B♭
F
No - bod - y knew from time to time if the plans

B♭
Gm
Gm (F bass)
C (E bass)
C
were changed, Oh, oh, oh, if the plans
F
Gm
F
Gm
were changed.
You can beat us with wires,
F
Gm
F
Gm
F
You can beat us with chain,
C
Dm
You can run lots of rules, but you know you can't out-run the his-to-ry train

Em
Dm
Gm
F
Gm
I seen a glo - ri - ous day, ai ee
F
C
ee
ee.
Dm
Dm
Dm
Ah

Gm
F
Bb
F
Four in the morn - in' I woke up from out of my dreams,
Bb
F
Bb
F
No - where to go but back to sleep, but I'm
Bb
Gm
Gm
(F bass)
rec - on - ciled, Oh, oh, oh,
C
(E bass)
C
Dm
I'm gon-na be up for a - while. Oh,

Gm
Gm
(F bass)
C
(E bass)
C
Dm
oh,
oh,
I'm gon-na be up for a - while.
Gm
G
(F bass)
C
(E bass)
C
Oh,
oh,
oh,
I'm gon-na be
Dm
up for a - while.
8va.

Papa Hobo

Moderately slow

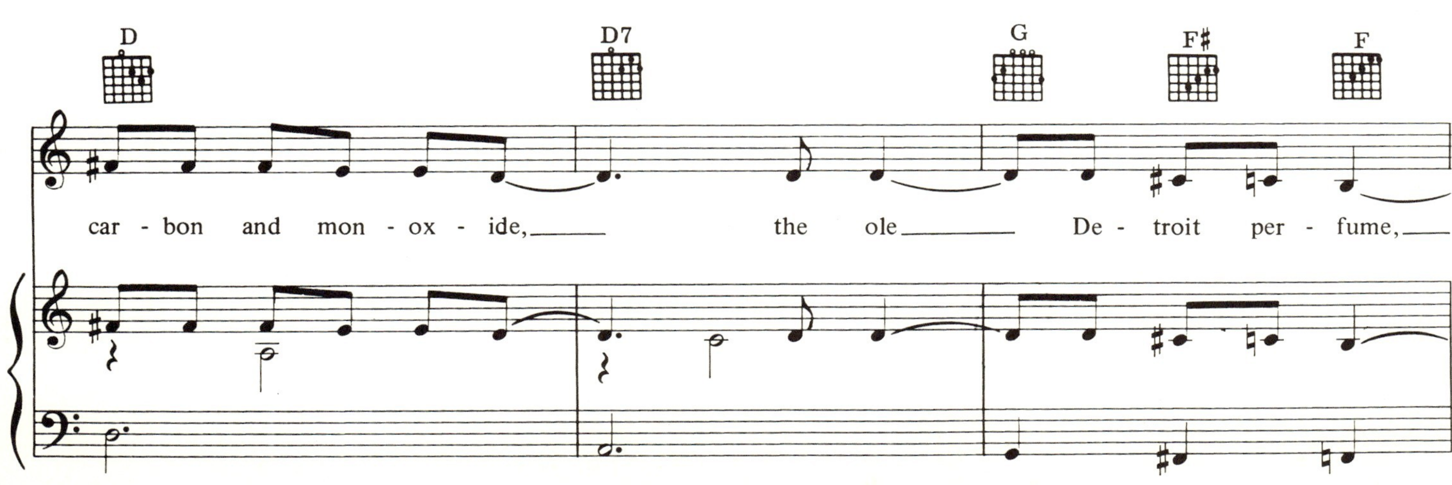

E
D
D7
G
It hangs on the high - ways in the morn - in', and it
A
D
E
A
lays you down by noon. Oh, Pa - pa Ho - bo, You can
G
G7
C
see that I'm dressed like a school boy, but I feel like a clown,
A
(C ♯bass)
G
E
C
It's a nat -'ral re - act - ion I learned in this bas -

Bm
Am
G
Bdim
Am
G
- ket - ball town.
Instrumental Solo
Am
G
Am
G
Am
G
Am
C
Sweep up,
I been
F
sweep - in' up the tips I've made.
I'm

C
Dm
C
liv - in' on ga - tor - ade,
G
G7
Plan - nin' my get - a - way.
3
C
De - troit, De - troit got a
F
hell of a hock - ey team, Got a

Em
Dm
E
(B bass)
Am
left - hand - ed way of mak - in' a man
Am
(G bass)
D
(F♯ bass)
G
sign up on that au - to - mo - tive dream, oh yeah,
G7
C7
C♯
oh yeah. Oh, Pa - pa,
3
D
G
F
Pa - pa Ho - bo, could you slip me a ride?

B♭ A A♭ G
Well, it's
F D (F♯ bass) G7 F G7
just af - ter break - fast, I'm in the road and the
C7 F Dm (A bass) B♭
weath - er man lied. Oo
Am B♭ Am Gm F
ah oo.
ritard.
p

Hobo's Blues

Moderately, with a bounce

F
D7
B♭
B♭m
F
D7
G7
C7
F
B♭7
G7
F
C7
F
F7

B♭
A7
A♭7
G7
3
F
D7
3
3
3
3
B♭
B♭m
F
D7
G7
C7
F
B♭7
G7
F
C7

F
F7
B♭
A7
A♭7
G7
F
D7
B♭
B♭m
F
D7

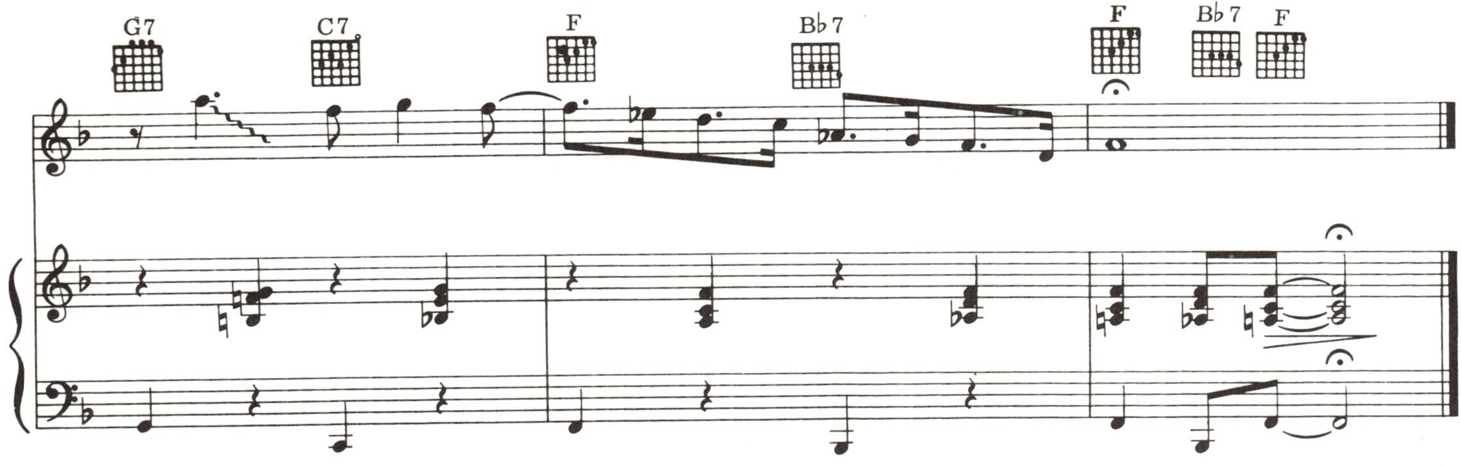
G7
C7
F
B♭7
F
B♭7
F

Paranoia Blues

Oh, no, no.
A
E
C♯m
There's on - ly one thing I need to know: Whose side
1. F♯7
B7
E
E
are you on?
I fly in - to J. F. K.
2. F♯7
B7
E
A
are you on, whose side are you on?
I got the Par - a - noi - a Blues from

E
3
knock - in' a - round in New York Cit - y, Where they
3
A
E
roll you for a nick - el, and they stick you for the ex - tra dime.
A
An - y way you choose, you're bound to lose in New York Cit -
E
A
B7
E
3
3
- y, Oh, I just got out in the nick of time. Well,
3
3
292

A
B7
E
No chord
I just got out in the nick of time.
Once I was down in Chi - na town,
E
E7
I was eat - in' some Lin's chow fon,
A
I hap - pened to turn a - round,
And when I
E
looked I seen my chow fon's gone.
Oh no, no,

Oh, no, no, There's
A E C♯m F♯ B
on - ly one thing I need to know: Whose side are you on, whose side are you on?
E B7
Well, there's on - ly one thing I need
E7 A F♯ B7 E
to know: Whose side, whose side, whose side?

Congratulations

E+
F
A
D
I don't know when,
oh, and I don't know
G
C
D
G
when,
oh, and I don't know when.
C
D
G
D
I no-tice so man-y peo-ple
D7
Em
C#7-5
C6
slip-pin' a-way,
And
3
3

Bm
Am
G
G (F bass)
C (E bass)
man - y more wait - ing in the lines in the
E+
F
A
D
court - rooms to - day, oh, in the
G
C
G
court - rooms to - - day.
G7
A
D
Love is not a game, love is not a toy, love's no ro -

G
C
G7
- mance.
A
D
G
Love will do you in, and love will wash you out, and need - less to say you
D
(F# bass)
Em
A7
D
won't stand a chance, and you won't stand a chance.
Em
Fm
A11
D
3
I'm hun - gry for learn - - in',
3

D
(C# bass)
D7
Em
C#m7-5
Won't you ans - wer me, please.
C6
Bm
Am
G
G
(F bass)
C
(E bass)
Can a man and a wo - man live to -
E+
F
A
D
geth - er in peace, oh, live to-geth-er in peace?
G
C
D
G
ritard.

Lyrics

TOM AND JERRY

Hey, Schoolgirl

Hey, Schoolgirl in the second row,
The teacher's looking over so I got to whisper
way down low,
To say, "Who-bop-a-loo-chi-bop, let's meet after
school at three."

She said, "Hey, babe, but there is
one thing more,
My school is over at half-past four,
Maybe when we're older then we can date,
Ooh, let's wait!"

Hey, Schoolgirl in the second row,
The teacher's looking over so I got to whisper
way down low,
To say, "Who-bop-a-loo-chi-bop, let's meet after
school at three."

She said, "Hey babe, I got a lot to do,
It takes me hours till my homework's through,
Someday we'll go steady, so don't you fret,
Ooh, not yet!"

Hey, Schoolgirl in the second row,
The teacher's looking over so I got to whisper
way down low,
To say, "Who-bop-a-loo-chi-bop, let's meet after
school at three."

Then she turned around to me with that
gleam in her eye,
She said, "I'm sorry if I passed you by,
I'm gonna skip my homework, gonna
cut my class,
Bug out of here real fast."

Hey, Schoolgirl in the second row,
Now we're going steady, hear the words that
I want you to know.
Well, it's "Who-bop-a-loo-chi-bop,
You're mine, I knew it all the time.
Who bop-a-loo-chi-bop, hah, you're mine."

A Church Is Burning

A Church Is Burning the flames rise higher
Like hands that are praying aglow in the sky
Like hands that are praying the fire is saying,
"You can burn down my churches but I
shall be free."

Three hooded men through the back roads did
creep
Torches in their hands while the
village lies asleep
Down to the church where just hours before
voices were singing and
Hands were beating and saying I won't be
a slave any more.
And A Church Is Burning the flames rise higher
Like hands that are praying aglow in the sky
Like hands that are praying the fire is saying,
"You can burn down my churches but I
shall be free."

Three hooded men, their hands lit the spark
Then they faded in the night and they vanished
in the dark
And in the cold light of morning there's
nothing that remains
But the ashes of a Bible and a can of kerosene.
And A Church Is Burning the flames rise higher
Like hands that are praying aglow in the sky
Like hands that are praying the fire is saying,
"You can burn down my churches but I
shall be free."

A church is more than just timber and stone
And freedom is a dark road when you're
walking it alone,
But the future is now and it's time
to take a stand
So the lost bells of freedom can ring out
in my land.
And A Church Is Burning the flames rise higher
Like hands that are praying aglow in the sky
Like hands that are praying the fire is saying,
"You can burn down my churches but I
shall be free."

You Don't Know Where Your Interest Lies

You don't know that you love me,
You don't know but I know that you do.
You may think that you are above me, yeah.
What you think isn't always true.

Don't try to debate me,
You should know that I'm womanly wise.
Still you try to manipulate me,
You Don't Know Where Your Interest Lies.

No, You Don't Know Where Your Interest Lies.
You don't begin to comprehend.

You're just a game I like to play.
You may think that we're friends all right,
But I won't let friendship get in my way,
No, I won't let friendship get in my way.

Indications indicate running the same riff will
turn you around.
Obviously you're going to blow it,
But you don't know it.

Red Rubber Ball

I should have know you'd bid me farewell.
There's a lesson to be learned from this
And I learned it very well.
Now I know you're not the only starfish
in the sea.
If I never hear your name again
It's all the same to me.

And I think it's gonna be all right.
Yeah, the worst is over,
Now the morning sun is shining like a
Red Rubber Ball.

You never cared for secrets I'd confide.
For you I'm just an ornament,
Something for your pride.
Always running, never caring, that's the
life you live.
Stolen minutes of your time
Were all you had to give.

And I think it's gonna be all right.
Yeah, the worst is over,
Now the morning sun is shining like a
Red Rubber Ball.

The story's in the past with nothing to recall.
I've got my life to live
And I don't need you at all.
The roller coaster ride we took is nearly
at an end.
I bought my ticket with my tears,
That's all I'm gonna spend.

And I think it's gonna be all right.
Yeah, the worst is over,
Now the morning sun is shining like a
Red Rubber Ball.

WEDNESDAY MORNING, 3 A.M.

The Sound Of Silence

Hello darkness, my old friend,
I've come to talk with you again,
Because a vision softly creeping,
Left its seeds while I was sleeping,
And the vision that was planted in my brain
Still remains
Within The Sound Of Silence.

In restless dreams I walked alone
Narrow streets of cobblestone,
'Neath the halo of a street lamp,
I turned my collar to the cold and damp
When my eyes were stabbed by the flash of
a neon light
That split the night
And touched The Sound Of Silence.

And in the naked light I saw
Ten thousand people, maybe more.
People talking without speaking,
People hearing without listening,
People writing songs that voices never share
And no one dare
Disturb The Sound Of Silence.

"Fools" said I, "You do not know
Silence like a cancer grows.
Hear my words that I might teach you,
Take my arms that I might reach you."
But my words like silent raindrops fell,
And echoed
In the wells of silence

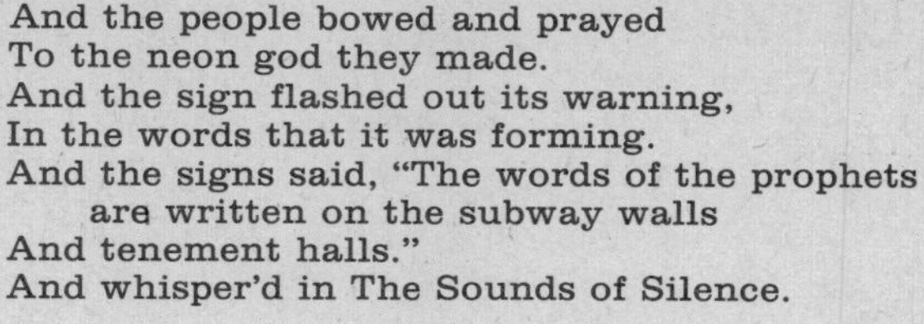

And the people bowed and prayed
To the neon god they made.
And the sign flashed out its warning,
In the words that it was forming.
And the signs said, "The words of the prophets
are written on the subway walls
And tenement halls."
And whisper'd in The Sounds of Silence.

Sparrow

Who will love a little Sparrow
Who's traveled far and cries for rest?
"Not I," said the oak tree,
"I won't share my branches with
no sparrow's nest,
And my blanket of leaves won't warm
her cold breast."

Who will love a little Sparrow
And who will speak a kindly word?
"Not I," said the swan,
"The entire idea is utterly absurd,
I'd be laughed at and scorned if the
other swans heard."

Who will take pity in his heart,
And who will feed a starving sparrow?
"Not I," said the golden wheat,
"I would if I could but I cannot I know,
I need all my grain to prosper and grow."

Who will love a little Sparrow?
Will no one write her eulogy?
"I will," said the earth,
"For all I've created returns unto me,
From dust were ye made and dust ye shall be."

Wednesday Morning, 3 A.M.

I can hear the soft breathing
Of the girl that I love,
As she lies here beside me
Asleep with the night,
And her hair, in a fine mist
Floats on my pillow,
Reflecting the glow
Of the winter moonlight.

She is soft, she is warm,
But my heart remains heavy,
And I watch as her breasts
Gently rise, gently fall,
For I know with the first light of dawn
I'll be leaving,
And tonight will be
All I have left to recall.

Oh, what have I done,
Why have I done it,
I've committed a crime,
I've broken the law.
For twenty-five dollars
And pieces of silver,
I held up and robbed
A hard liquor store.

My life seems unreal,
My crime an illusion,
A scene badly written
In which I must play.
Yet I know as I gaze
At my young love beside me,
The morning is just a few hours away.

SOUNDS OF SILENCE

I Am A Rock

A winter's day
In a deep and dark December;
I am alone,
Gazing from my window to the streets below
On a freshly fallen silent shroud of snow.
I Am A Rock,
I am an island.

I've built walls,
A fortress deep and mighty,
That none may penetrate.
I have no need of friendship;
friendship causes pain.
It's laughter and it's loving I disdain.
I Am A Rock,
I am an island.

Don't talk of love,
But I've heard the words before;
It's sleeping in my memory.
I won't disturb the slumber of feelings
that have died.
If I never loved I never would have cried.
I Am A Rock,
I am an island.

I have my books
And my poetry to protect me;
I am shielded in my armor,
Hiding in my room, safe within my womb.
I touch no one and no one touches me.
I Am A Rock,
I am an island.

And a rock feels no pain;
And an island never cries.

Leaves That Are Green

I was twenty-one years when I wrote this song.
I'm twenty-two now but I won't be for long
Time hurries on.
And the Leaves That Are Green turn to brown,
And they wither with the wind,
And they crumble in your hand.

Once my heart was filled with the love of a girl.
I held her close, but she faded in the night
Like a poem I meant to write.
And the Leaves That Are Green turn to brown,
And they wither with the wind,
And they crumble in your hand.

I threw a pebble in a brook
And watched the ripples run away
And they never made a sound.
And the Leaves That Are Green turned to brown,
And they wither with the wind,
And they crumble in your hand.

Hello, Hello, Hello, Good-bye,
Good-bye, Good-bye, Good-bye,
That's all there is.
And the Leaves That Are Green turned to brown,
And they wither with the wind,
And they crumble in your hand.

Blessed

Blessed are the meek for they shall inherit.
Blessed is the lamb whose blood flows.
Blessed are the sat upon, Spat upon, Ratted on.
O Lord, Why have you forsaken me?
I got no place to go,
I've walked around Soho for the last night or so.
Ah, but it doesn't matter, no.

Blessed is the land and the kingdom.
Blessed is the man whose soul belongs to.
Blessed are the meth drinkers, Pot sellers,
Illusion dwellers.
O Lord, Why have you forsaken me?
My words trickle down, like a wound
That I have no intention to heal.

Blessed are the stained glass.
window pane glass.
Blessed is the church service
makes me nervous.
Blessed are the penny rookers, Cheap hookers,
Groovy lookers.
O Lord, Why have you forsaken me?
I have tended my own garden
Much too long.

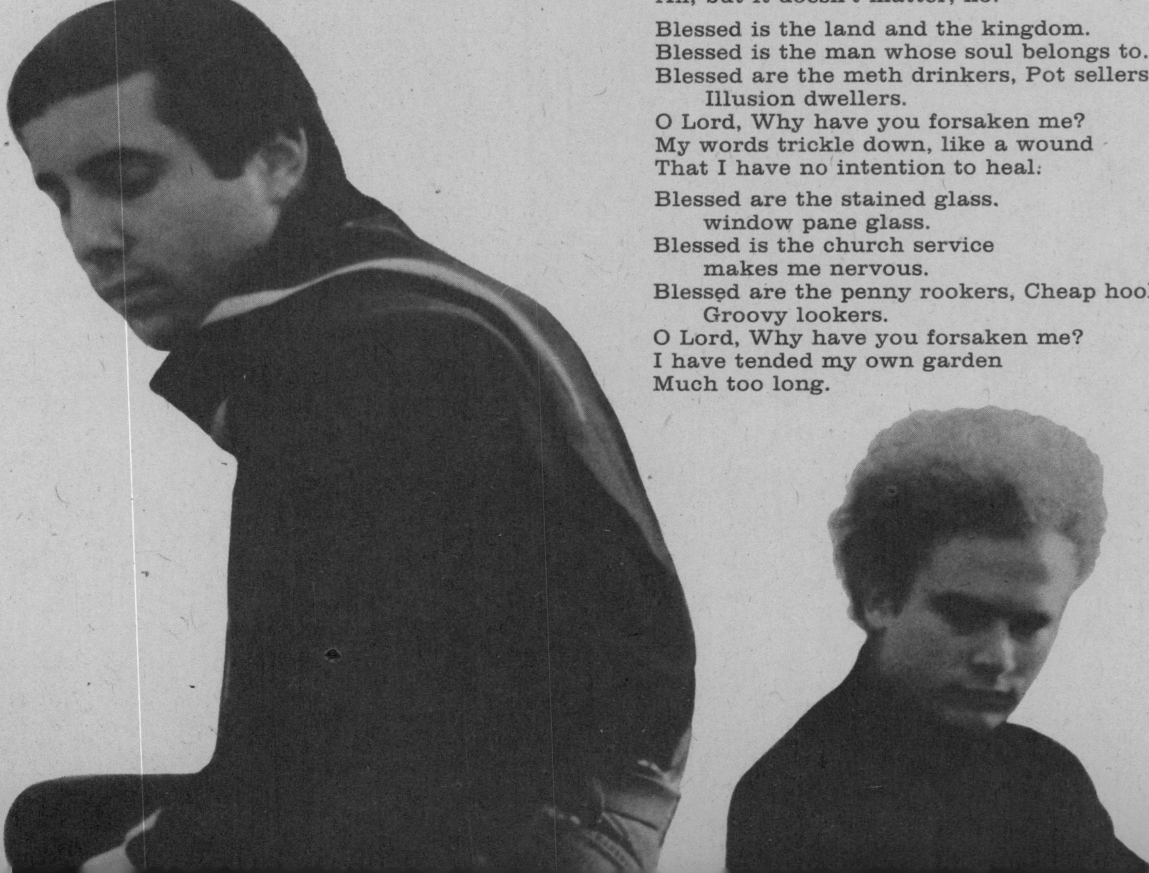

Kathy's Song

I hear the drizzle of the rain
Like a memory it falls
Soft and warm continuing
Tapping on my roof and walls.

And from the shelter of my mind
Through the window of my eyes
I gaze beyond the rain-drenched streets
To England where my heart lies.

My mind's distracted and diffused
My thoughts are many miles away
They lie with you when you're asleep
And kiss you when you start your day.

And a song I was writing is left undone
I don't know why I spend my time
Writing songs I can't believe
With words that tear and strain to rhyme.

And so you see I have come to doubt
All that I once held as true
I stand alone without beliefs
The only truth I know is you.

And as I watch the drops of rain
Weave their weary paths and die
I know that I am like the rain
There but for the grace of you go I.

Somewhere They Can't Find Me

I can hear the soft breathing of the
girl that I love,
As she lies here beside me
asleep with the night.
Her hair in a fine mist floats on my pillow,
Reflecting the glow of the winter moonlight.

But I've got to creep down the alley way,
Fly down the highway,
Before they come to catch me I'll be gone.
Somewhere They Can't Find Me.

Oh baby, you don't know what I've done,
I've committed a crime, I've broken the law.
While you were here sleeping and just
dreaming of me,
I held up and robbed a liquor store.

But I've got to creep down the alley way,
Fly down the highway,
Before they come to catch me I'll be gone.
Somewhere They Can't Find Me.

Oh my life seems unreal, my crime an illusion,
A scene badly written in which I must play.
And though it puts me up tight to leave you,
I know it's not right to leave you,
When morning is just a few hours away.

But I've got to creep down the alley way,
Fly down the highway,
Before they come to catch me I'll be gone.
Somewhere They Can't Find Me.

Richard Cory

They say that Richard Cory owns one half
of this whole town,
With political connections to spread
his wealth around.
Born into society, a banker's only child,
He had everything a man could want:
power, grace and style.

But I work in his factory
And I curse the life I'm living
And I curse my poverty
And I wish that I could be,
Oh, I wish that I could be,
Oh, I wish that I could be
Richard Cory.

The papers print his picture almost
everywhere he goes:
Richard Cory at the opera, Richard Cory
at a show.
And the rumor of his parties and the
orgies on his yacht!
Oh, he surely must be happy with
everything he's got.

But I work in his factory
And I curse the life I'm living
And I curse my poverty
And I wish that I could be,
Oh, I wish that I could be,
Oh, I wish that I could be
Richard Cory.

He freely gave to charity, he had
the common touch,
And they were grateful for his patronage and
thanked him very much,
So my mind was filled with wonder when the
evening headlines read:
"Richard Cory went home last night and
put a bullet through his head."

But I work in his factory
And I curse the life I'm living
And I curse my poverty
And I wish that I could be,
Oh, I wish that I could be,
Oh, I wish that I could be
Richard Cory.

We've Got A Groovy Thing Goin'

Bad news, bad news!
I heard you're packing to leave!
I come arunning right over;
I just couldn't believe it,
I just couldn't believe it.

Oh, baby, baby,
You must be out of your mind.
Do you know what you're kicking away?
We've Got A Groovy Thing Goin', baby,
We've got a groovy thing.

I never done you no wrong,
I never hit you when you're down,
I always gave you good loving,
I never ran around,
I never ran around.

Oh, baby, baby,
You must be out of your mind.
Do you know what you're kicking away?
We've Got A Groovy Thing Goin', baby,
We've got a groovy thing.

There's something you ought to know
If you're fixing to go,
I can't make it without you;
No no no no, no, no, no, no,
No no no no, no, no, no.

Oh, baby, baby,
You must be out of your mind.
Do you know what you're kicking away?
We've Got A Groovy Thing Goin', baby,
We've got a groovy thing.

We've Got A Groovy Thing Goin', baby,
We've got a groovy thing.

A Most Peculiar Man

He was A Most Peculiar Man.
That's what Mrs. Riordan said
and she should know;
She lived upstairs from him
She said he was A Most Peculiar Man.

He was A Most Peculiar Man.
He lived all alone within a house,
Within a room, within himself,
A Most Peculiar Man.

He had no friends, he seldom spoke
And no one in turn ever spoke to him,
'Cause he wasn't friendly and he didn't care
And he wasn't like them.
Oh, no! he was A Most Peculiar Man.

He died last Saturday.
He turned on the gas and he went to sleep
With the windows closed so he'd never wake up
To his silent world and his tiny room;
And Mrs. Riordan says he has
a brother somewhere
Who should be notified soon.
And all the people said, "What a shame
that he's dead,
But wasn't he A Most Peculiar Man?"

April Come She Will

April Come She Will
When streams are ripe and swelled with rain;
May, she will stay,
Resting in my arms again.

June, she'll change her tune,
In restless walks she'll prowl the night;
July, she will fly
And give no warning to her flight.

August, die she must,
The autumn winds blow chilly and cold;
September I'll remember.
A love once new has now grown old.

PARSLEY, SAGE, ROSEMARY AND THYME

Scarborough Fair/Canticle

Are you going to Scarborough Fair:
Parsley, sage, rosemary and thyme.
Remember me to one who lives there.
She once was a true love of mine.

On the side of a hill in the deep forest green.
Tracing of sparrow on snow-crested brown.
Blankets and bedclothes the
child of the mountain
Sleeps unaware of the clarion call.

Tell her to make me a cambric shirt:
Parsley, sage, rosemary and thyme;
Without no seams nor needle work,
Then she'll be a true love of mine.

On the side of a hill a sprinkling of leaves.
Washes the grave with silvery tears.
A soldier cleans and polishes a gun.
Sleeps unaware of the clarion call.

Tell her to find me an acre of land:
Parsley, sage, rosemary and thyme;
Between the salt water and the sea strand,
Then she'll be a true love of mine.

War bellows blazing in scarlet battalions.
Generals order their soldiers to kill.
And to fight for a cause they've
long ago forgotten.

Tell her to reap it with a sickle of leather:
Parsley, sage, rosemary and thyme;
And gather it all in a bunch of heather,
Then she'll be a true love of mine.

Patterns

The night sets softly
With the hush of falling leaves,
Casting shivering shadows
On the houses through the trees,
And the light from a street lamp
Paints a pattern on my wall,
Like the pieces of a puzzle
Or a child's uneven scrawl.

Up a narrow flight of stairs
In a narrow little room,
As I lie upon by bed
In the early evening gloom.
Impaled on my wall
My eyes can dimly see
The pattern of my life
And the puzzle that is me.

From the moment of my birth
To the instant of my death,
There are Patterns I must follow
Just as I must breathe each breath.
Like a rat in a maze
The path before me lies,
And the pattern never alters
Until the rat dies.

And the pattern still remains
On the wall where darkness fell,
And it's fitting that it should,
For in darkness I must dwell.
Like the color of my skin,
Or the day that I grow old,
My life is made of Patterns
That can scarcely be controlled.

Cloudy

Cloudy
The sky is gray and white and Cloudy,
Sometimes I think it's hanging down on me.
And it's a hitchhike a hundred miles.
I'm a rag-a-muffin child.
Pointed finger-painted smile.
I left my shadow waiting down the
road for me a while.

Cloudy
My thoughts are scattered and they're Cloudy,
They have no borders, no boundaries.
They echo and they swell.
From Tolstoi to Tinker Bell.
Down from Berkeley to Carmel.
Got some pictures in my pocket and a lot
of time to kill.

Hey sunshine
I haven't seen you in a long time.
Why don't you show your face and
bend my mind?
These clouds stick to the sky
Like floating questions, why?
And they linger there to die.
They don't know where they are going, and,
my friend, neither do I.

Cloudy,
Cloudy.

Homeward Bound

I'm sitting in the railway station,
Got a ticket for my destination.
On a tour of one-night stands my suitcase
and guitar in hand
And ev'ry stop is neatly planned for a poet
and a one-man band.
Homeward Bound,
I wish I was,
Homeward Bound.
Home where my thought's escaping,
Home where my music's playing,
Home where my love lies waiting
Silently for me.

Ev'ry day's an endless stream
Of cigarettes and magazines.
And each town looks the same to me, the
movies and the factories
And ev'ry stranger's face I see reminds me
that I long to be,
Homeward Bound,
I wish I was,
Homeward Bound.
Home where my thought's escaping,
Home where my music's playing,
Home where my love lies waiting
Silently for me.

Tonight I'll sing my songs again,
I'll play the game and pretend.
But all my words come back to me in
shades of mediocrity
Like emptiness in harmony I need someone
to comfort me.
Homeward Bound,
I wish I was,
Homeward Bound.
Home where my thought's escaping,
Home where my music's playing,
Home where my love lies waiting
Silently for me.

The Big Bright Green Pleasure Machine

Do people have a tendency to dump on you?
Does your group have more
cavities than theirs?
Do all the hippies seem to get the jump on you?
Do you sleep alone when others sleep in pairs?
Well there's no need to complain,
We'll eliminate your pain.
We can neutralize your brain.
You'll feel just fine
Now.
Buy a Big Bright Green Pleasure Machine!

Do figures of authority just shoot you down?
Is life within the business world a drag?
Did your boss just mention that you'd
better shop around
To find yourself a more productive bag?
Are you worried and distressed?
Can't seem to get no rest?
Put our product to the test.
You'll feel just fine
Now.
Buy a Big Bright Green Pleasure Machine!

You better hurry up and order one.
Our limited supply is very nearly gone.
Do you nervously await the blows of cruel fate?
Do your checks bounce higher
than a rubber ball?
Are you worried 'cause your girlfriend's
just a little late?
Are you looking for a way to chuck it all?
We can end your daily strife
At a reasonable price.
You've seen it advertised in **Life**.
You'll feel just fine
Now.
Buy a Big Bright Green Pleasure Machine!

A Simple Desultory Philippic (Or How I Was Robert McNamara'd Into Submission)

I been Norman Mailered, Maxwell Taylored.
I been John O'Hara'd, McNamara'd.
I been Rolling Stoned and Beatled till I'm blind.
I been Ayn Randed, nearly branded
Communist, 'cause I'm left-handed.
That's the hand I use, well, never mind!

I been Phil Spectored, resurrected.
I been Lou Adlered, Barry Sadlered.
Well, I paid all the dues I want to pay.
And I learned the truth from Lenny Bruce,
And all my wealth won't buy me health,
So I smoke a pint of tea a day.

I knew a man, his brain so small,
He couldn't think of nothing at all.
He's not the same as you and me.
He doesn't dig poetry. He's so unhip that
When you say Dylan, he thinks you're talking
about Dylan Thomas,
Whoever he was.
The man ain't got no culture,
But its alright, ma,
Everybody must get stoned.

I been Mick Jaggered, silver daggered.
Andy Warhol, won't you please come home?
I been mothered, fathered, aunt and uncled,
Been Roy Haleed and Art Garfunkeled.
I just discovered somebody's tapped my phone.

The 59th Street Bridge Song (Feelin' Groovy)

Slow down, you move too fast.
You got to make the morning last.
Just kicking down the cobble stones,
Looking for fun and Feelin' Groovy.

Hello lampost,
What cha knowing?
I've come to watch your flowers growing.
Ain't cha got no rhymes for me?
Doot-in' doo-doo,
Feelin' Groovy.

Got no deeds to do,
No promises to keep.
I'm dappled and drowsy and ready to sleep.
Let the morning time drop all its petals on me.
Life, I love you,
All is groovy.

The Dangling Conversation

It's a still life water color,
Of a now late afternoon,
As the sun shines through the curtained lace
And shadows wash the room.
And we sit and drink our coffee
Couched in our indifference,
Like shells upon the shore
You can hear the ocean roar
In The Dangling Conversation
And the superficial sighs,
The borders of our lives.

And you read your Emily Dickinson,
And I my Robert Frost,
And we note our place with bookmarkers
That measure what we've lost.
Like a poem poorly written
We are verses out of rhythm,
Couplets out of rhyme,
In syncopated time
And The Dangling Conversation
And the superficial sighs
Are the borders of our lives.

Yes, we speak of things that matter,
With words that must be said,
"Can analysis be worthwhile?"
"Is the theater really dead?"
And how the room is softly faded
And I only kiss your shadow,
I cannot feel your hand,
You're a stranger now unto me
Lost in The Dangling Conversation
And the superfical sighs
In the borders of our lives.

Flowers Never Bend With The Rainfall

Through the corridors of sleep
Past the shadows dark and deep
My mind dances and leaps in confusion.
I don't know what is real,
I can't touch what I feel
And I hide behind the shield of my illusion.

So I'll continue to continue to pretend
My life will never end,
And Flowers Never Bend
With The Rainfall.

The mirror on my wall
Casts an image dark and small
But I'm not sure at all it's my reflection.
I am blinded by the light
Of God and truth and right
And I wander in the night without direction.

So I'll continue to continue to pretend
My life will never end,
And Flowers Never Bend
With The Rainfall.

It's no matter if you're born
To play the King or pawn
For the line is thinly drawn 'tween
joy and sorrow,
So my fantasy
Becomes reality,
And I must be what I must be
and face tomorrow.

So I'll continue to continue to pretend
My life will never end,
And Flowers Never Bend
With The Rainfall.

For Emily, Whenever I May Find Her

What a dream I had:
Pressed in organdy;
Clothed in crinoline of smoky Burgundy;
Softer than the rain.
I wandered empty streets
Down past the shop displays.
I heard cathedral bells
Tripping down the alley ways,
As I walked on.

And when you ran to me
Your cheeks flushed with the night.
We walked on frosted fields of
juniper and lamplight,
I held your hand.
And when I awoke and felt you warm and near,
I kissed your honey hair with my grateful tears.
Oh I love you, girl.
Oh, I love you.

A Poem On The Underground Wall

The last train is nearly due,
The underground is closing soon,
And in the dark deserted station,
Restless in anticipation,
A man waits in the shadows.

His restless eyes leap and scratch,
At all that they can touch or catch,
And hidden deep within his pocket,
Safe within its silent socket,
He holds a colored crayon.

Now from the tunnel's stony womb,
The carriage rides to meet the groom,
And opens wide and welcome doors,
But he hesitates, then withdraws
Deeper in the shadows.

And the train is gone suddenly
On wheels clicking silently
Like a gently tapping litany,
And he holds his crayon rosary
Tighter in his hand.

Now from his pocket quick he flashes,
The crayon on the wall he slashes,
Deep upon the advertising,
A single worded poem comprised
Of four letters.

And his heart is laughing, screaming, pounding,
The poem across the tracks rebounding,
Shadowed by the exit light
His legs take their ascending flight
To seek the breast of darkness and be suckled
by the night.

7 o'clock News/Silent Night

This is the early evening edition of the news.
The recent fight in the House of Representatives was over the open housing section of the Civil Rights Bill.
Brought traditional enemies together but it left the defenders of the measure without the votes of their strongest supporters.
President Johnson originally proposed an outright ban covering discrimination by everyone for every type of housing but it had no chance from the start and everyone in Congress knew it.
A compromise was painfully worked out in the House Judiciary Committee.
In Los Angeles today comedian Lenny Bruce died of what was believed to be an overdose of narcotics.
Bruce was 42 years old.
Dr. Martin Luther King says he does not intend to cancel plans for an open housing march Sunday into the Chicago suburb of Cicero.
Cook County Sheriff Richard Ogleby asked King to call off the march and the police in Cicero said they would ask the National Guard be called out if it is held.
King now in Atlanta, Georgia, plans to return to Chicago Tuesday.

In Chicago Richard Speck, accused murderer of nine student nurses, was brought before a grand jury today for indictment.
The nurses were found stabbed and strangled in their Chicago apartment.
In Washington the atmosphere was tense today as a special subcommittee of the House Committee on Un-American activities continued its probe into anti-Viet Nam war protests.
Demonstrators were forcibly evicted from the hearings when they began chanting anti-war slogans.
Former Vice-President Richard Nixon says that unless there is a substantial increase in the present war effort in Viet Nam, the U.S. should look forward to five more years of war.
In a speech before the Convention of the Veterans of Foreign Wars in New York, Nixon also said opposition to the war in this country is the greatest single weapon working against the U.S.
That's the 7 o'clock edition of the news.
Goodnight.

Silent Night
Holy night
All is calm
All is bright
Round yon virgin mother and child
Holy infant so tender and mild
Sleep in heavenly peace, sleep in heavenly peace.

BOOKENDS

Mrs. Robinson

And here's to you, Mrs. Robinson,
Jesus loves you more than you will know,
(Wo, wo, wo.)
God bless you, please, Mrs. Robinson,
Heaven holds a place for those who pray,
(Hey, hey, hey, hey, hey, hey.)

We'd like to know
A little bit about you
For our files.
We'd like to help you learn
To help yourself.
Look around you, all you see
Are sympathetic eyes,
Stroll around the grounds
Until you feel at home.

And here's to you, Mrs. Robinson,
Jesus loves you more than you will know,
(Wo, wo, wo.)
God bless you, please, Mrs. Robinson,
Heaven holds a place for those who pray,
(Hey, hey, hey, hey, hey, hey.)

Hide it in a hiding place
Where no one ever goes,
Put it in your pantry with your cupcakes,
It's a little secret,
Just the Robinsons' affair,
Most of all, you've got to hide it
From the kids.
Coo, coo, ca-choo, Mrs. Robinson,
Jesus loves you more than you will know,
(Wo, wo, wo.)
God bless you, please, Mrs. Robinson,
Heaven holds a place for those who pray.
(Hey, hey, hey, hey, hey, hey.)

Sitting on a sofa
On a Sunday afternoon,
Going to the candidates' debate,
Laugh about it,
Shout about it,
When you've got to choose,
Ev'ry way you look at it, you lose.

Where have you gone, Joe DiMaggio?
A nation turns its lonely eyes to you,
(Woo, woo, woo.)
What's that you say, Mrs. Robinson?
"Joltin' Joe" has left and gone away.
(Hey, hey, hey, hey, hey, hey.)

Save The Life Of My Child

"Good God, Don't jump!"
A boy sat on the ledge,
An old man who had fainted was revived.
And ev'ryone agreed 'twould be a miracle indeed
If the boy survived.
"Save The Life Of My Child!"
Cried the desperate mother.
Ah, ah, ah, ah.

A woman from the supermarket
Ran to call the cops.
"He must be high on something," someone said.
Though it never made **The New York Times,**
In the **Daily News,** the caption read,
"Save The Life Of My Child!"
Cried the desperate mother.
Ah, ah, ah, ah.

A patrol car passing by
Halted to a stop.
Said officer McDougal in dismay,
"The force can't do a decent job
'Cause the kids got no respect
For the law today."
"Save The Life Of My Child!"
Cried the desperate mother.
"What's becoming of the children?"
People asking each other.
When darkness fell, excitement
kissed the crowd
And made them wild,
The atmosphere was freaky holiday.
When the spotlight hit the boy
And the crowd began to cheer,
He flew away!
Oh, my Grace, I got no hiding place.

America

"Let us be lovers,
We'll marry our fortunes together.
I've got some real estate
Here in my bag."
So we bought a pack of cigarettes,
And Mrs. Wagner's pies,
And walked off
To look for America.
"Kathy," I said,
As we boarded a Greyhound in Pittsburgh,
"Michigan seems like a dream to me now.
It took me four days
To hitchhike from Saginaw.
I've come to look for America."

Laughing on the bus,
Playing games with the faces,
She said the man in the gabardine suit
Was a spy.
I said, "Be careful,
His bowtie is really a camera."
"Toss me a cigarette,
I think there's one in my raincoat."
"We smoked the last one
An hour ago."

So I looked at the scenery,
She read her magazine;
And the moon rose over an open field.
"Kathy, I'm lost," I said,
Though I knew she was sleeping.
"I'm empty and aching and
I don't know why."
Counting the cars
On the New Jersey Turnpike.
They've all come
To look for America,
All come to look for America.
All come to look for America.

Overs

Why don't we stop fooling ourselves?
The game is over,
Over,
Over.
No good times, no bad times
There's no times at all
Just **The New York Times**
Sittin' on the window sill
Near the flowers.

We might as well be apart
It hardly matters,
We sleep sep'rately
And drop a smile passing in the hall
But there's no laughs left
'Cause we laughed them all,
And we laughed them all
In a very short time.

Time is tapping on my forehead
Hanging from my mirror
Rattling the teacups.

And I wonder how long
Can I delay?
We're just a habit like saccharine
And I'm habitually feeling kinda blue,
But each time I try on the thought
of leaving you
I stop!
I stop and think it over.

Old Friends

Old Friends,
Old Friends,
Sat on their park bench
Like bookends.
A newspaper blown through the grass
Falls on the round toes
Of the high shoes
Of the Old Friends.

Old Friends,
Winter companions,
The old men
Lost in their overcoats,
Waiting for the sunset.
The sounds of the city,
Sifting through trees,
Settle like dust
On the shoulders
Of the Old Friends.

Can you imagine us
Years from today,
Sharing a park bench quietly?
How terribly strange
To be seventy.

Old Friends,
Memory brushes the same years.
Silently sharing the same fears.

Bookends

Time it was,
And what a time it was,
It was . . .
A time of innocence,
A time of confidences.
Long ago,
It must be . . .
I have a photograph
Preserve your memories;
They're all that's left you.

Fakin' It

When she goes, she's gone,
If she stays, she stays here.
The girl does what she wants to do,
She knows what she wants to do
And I know I'm Fakin' It,
I'm not really makin' it.

I'm such a dubious soul
And a walk in the garden
Wears me down.
Tangled in the fallen vines,
Picking up the punch lines,
I've just been Fakin' It,
Not really makin' it.
No, no, no, no.

Is there any danger?
No, no, not really,
Just lean on me.
Take the time to treat
Your friendly neighbors honestly,
I've just been Fakin' It, Fakin' It,
Not really makin' it;
This feelin' of Fakin' It,
I still haven't shaken it.
Prior to this lifetime
I surely was a tailor.
Look at me.

Good morning, Mr. Leach,
Have you had a busy day?
I own the tailor's face and hands,
I am the tailor's face and hands.
I know I'm Fakin' It, Fakin' It,
I'm not really makin' it,
This feelin' of Fakin' It,
I still haven't shaken it, shaken it.
I know I'm Fakin' It,
I'm not really makin' it.

Punky's Dilemma

Wish I was a Kellogg's Cornflake
Floating in my bowl taking movies.
Relaxing awhile living in style
Talking to a raisin who occasionally plays L.A.
Casually glancing at his toupee.

Wish I was an English muffin
About to make the most out of a toaster.
I'd ease myself down,
Coming up brown
I prefer boysenberry
More than any ordinary jam.
I'm a citizens for boysenberry jam fan.

Ah, South California.
If I become a first lieutenant
Would you put my photo on your piano?
To Mary Jane
Best wishes, Martin.
Old Roger, draft-dodger
Leaving by the basement door.
Ev'rybody knows what he's
Tippy-toeing down there for.

A Hazy Shade Of Winter

Time,
Time,
Time, see what's become of me,
While I looked around for my possibilities,
I was so hard to please,
But look around,
Leaves are brown
And the sky is A Hazy Shade Of Winter.

Hear the Salvation Army Band,
Down by the riverside,
It's bound to be a better ride,
Than what you've got planned,
Carry your cup in your hand,
And look around,
Leaves are brown now,
And the sky is A Hazy Shade Of Winter.

Hang on to your hopes, my friend,
That's an easy thing to say,
But if your hopes should pass away,
Simply pretend that you can build them again.
Look around;
The grass is high,
The fields are ripe:
It's the springtime of my life.

Seasons change with the scenery,
Weaving time in a tapestry.
Won't you stop and remember me,
At any convenient time?
Funny how my mem'ry skips,
While looking over manuscripts
Of unpublished rhyme,
Drinking my vodka and lime.
I look around,
Leaves are brown now,
And the sky is A Hazy Shade Of Winter.

Look around;
Leaves are brown,
There's a patch of snow on the ground.

At The Zoo

Someone told me,
It's all happening At The Zoo.
I do believe it,
I do believe it's true.

It's a light and tumble journey,
From the East Side to the park.
Just a fine and fancy ramble
To the zoo.
But you can take the crosstown bus,
If it's raining or it's cold,
And the animals will love it,
If you do, if you do.
Something tells me,
It's all happening At The Zoo.
I do believe it,
I do believe it's true.

The monkeys stand for honesty,
Giraffes are insincere,
And the elephants are kindly, but
They're dumb.
Orangutans are skeptical
Of changes in their cages,
And the zookeeper is very fond of rum.
Zebras are reactionaries,
Antelopes are missionaries,
Pigeons plot in secrecy,
And hamsters turn on frequently.
What a gas! You gotta come and see
At The Zoo.

BRIDGE OVER TROUBLED WATER

Cecilia

Celia, you're breaking my heart,
you're shaking my confidence daily.
Oh, Cecilia, I'm down on my knees,
I'm begging you please to come home.

Celia, you're breaking my heart,
You're shaking my confidence daily.
Oh, Cecilia, I'm down on my knees,
I'm begging you please to come home.
Ho-ho-home.

Making love in the afternoon with Cecilia,
Up in my bedroom,
I got up to wash my face,
When I come back to bed,
Someone's taken my place.

Celia, you're breaking my heart,
You're shaking my confidence daily.
Oh, Cecilia, I'm down on my knees,
I'm begging you please to come home.
Come on home.

Jubilation,
She loves me again,
I fall on the floor and I'm laughing.

Jubilation
She loves me again,
I fall on the floor and I'm laughing.

Keep The Customer Satisfied

Gee, but it's great to be back home,
Home is where I want to be.
I've been on the road so long my friend,
And if you came along
I know you couldn't disagree.
It's the same old story
Ev'rywhere I go,
I get slandered,
Libeled,
I hear words I never heard
In the Bible.
And I'm one step ahead of the shoe shine,
Two steps away from the county line,
Just trying to keep my customers satisfied,
Satisfied.

Deputy Sheriff said to me,
"Tell me what you come here for, boy.
You better get your bags and flee.
You're in trouble boy,
And now you're heading into more."
It's the same old story
Ev'rywhere I go,
I get slandered,
Libeled,
I hear words I never heard
In the Bible.
And I'm one step ahead of the shoe shine,
Two steps away from the county line,
Just trying to keep my customers satisfied,
Satisfied.

But it's the same old story
Ev'rywhere I go,
I get slandered,
Libeled,
I hear words I never heard
In the Bible.
And I'm so tired,
I'm oh so tired,
But I'm trying to keep my customers satisfied,
Satisfied.

So Long, Frank Lloyd Wright

So Long, Frank Lloyd Wright.
I can't believe your song is gone so soon.
I barely learned the tune.
So soon,
So soon.

I'll remember Frank Lloyd Wright.
All of the nights we'd harmonize till dawn.
I never laughed so long.
So long,
So long.

Architects may come and
Architects may go and
Never change your point of view.
When I run dry
I stop awhile and think of you.

So Long, Frank Lloyd Wright.
All of the nights we'd harmonize till dawn.
I never laughed so long.
So long,
So long.

The Boxer

I am just a poor boy.
Though my story's seldom told,
I have squandered my resistance
For a pocketful of mumbles,
Such are promises.
All lies and jest,
Still a man hears what he wants to hear,
And disregards the rest.

When I left my home
And my family,
I was no more than a boy
In the company of strangers
In the quiet of the railway station
Running scared,
Laying low,
Seeking out the poorer quarters
Where the ragged people go,
Looking for the places
Only they would know.

Asking only workman's wages
I come looking for a job,
But I get no offers,
Just a come-on from the whores
on Seventh Avenue.
I do declare,
There were times when I was lonesome
I took some comfort there.

Then I'm laying out my winter clothes
And wishing I was gone,
Going home
Where the New York City winters
Aren't bleeding me,
Leading me,
Going home.

In the clearing stands a boxer,
And a fighter by his trade,
And he carries the reminders
Of ev'ry glove that laid him down
Or cut him till he cried out
In his anger and his shame,
"I am leaving, I am leaving."
But the fighter still remains.

Baby Driver

My daddy was the family bassman,
My mama was an engineer,
And I was born one dark gray morn
With music coming in my ears,
In my ears.
They call me Baby Driver,
And once upon a pair of wheels,
Hit the road and I'm gone.
What's my number,
I wonder how your engine feels.
Scoot down the road,
What's my number,
I wonder how your engine feels.

My daddy was a prominent frogman,
My mama's in the Naval reserve,
When I was young I carried a gun
But I never got the chance to serve,
I did not serve.

They call me Baby Driver,
And once upon a pair of wheels,
Hit the road and I'm gone.
What's my number,
I wonder how your engine feels.
Scoot down the road,
What's my number,
I wonder how your engine feels.

My daddy got a big promotion,
My mama got a raise in pay,
There's no one home, we're all alone
Oh, come into my room and play.
Yes, we can play.

I'm not talking about your pigtails,
But I'm talking 'bout your sex appeal,
Hit the road and I'm gone
What's my number,
I wonder how your engine feels.
Scoot down the road,
What's my number,
I wonder how your engine feels.

The Only Living Boy In New York

Tom, get your plane right on time.
I know your part'll go fine.
Fly down to Mexico.
Da-n-da-da-n-da-da-n-da-n and here I am,
The Only Living Boy In New York.
I get the news I need on the weather report.
I can gather all the news I need on
the weather report.
Hey, I've got nothing to do today but smile.
Da-n-da-da-n-do-da-n-do-n here I am,
The Only Living Boy In New York.

Half of the time we're gone but we
don't know where,
And we don't know where.

Tom, get your plane right on time.
I know that you've been eager to fly now.
Hey, let your honesty shine, shine, shine now,
Do-da-n-do-da-n-do-da-n-do
Like it shines on me.
The Only Living Boy In New York.
The Only Living Boy In New York.

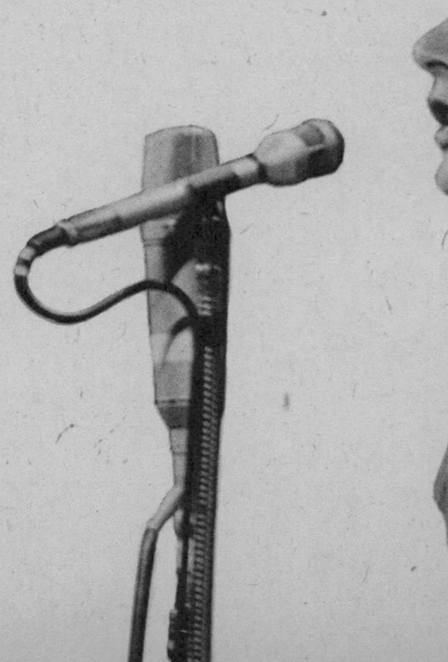

Why Don't You Write Me?

Why Don't You Write Me?
I'm out in the jungle,
I'm hungry to hear you.
Send me a card,
I am waiting so hard
To be near you.
(La la la.)
Why don't you write?
Something is wrong
And I know I got to be there.
Maybe I'm lost,
But I can't make the cost
Of the airfare.
Tell me why
Why
Why
Tell me why
Why
Why
Why Don't You Write Me?
A letter would brighten
My loneliest evening.
Mail it today
If it's only to say
That you're leaving me.
(La la la.)
Monday morning, sitting in the sun
Hoping and wishing for the mail to come.
Tuesday, never got a word, mmm.
Wednesday, Thursday, ain't no sign,
Drank a half bottle of iodine.
Friday, woe is me,
I'm gonna hang my body from the highest tree.
Why Don't You Write Me?
Why Don't You Write Me?

Song For The Asking

Here is my Song For The Asking,
Ask me and I will play
So sweetly, I'll make you smile;
This is my tune for the taking,
Take it, don't turn away
I've been waiting all my life.
Thinking it over, I've been sad,
Thinking it over, I'd be more than glad
To change my ways for the asking,
Ask me and I will play
All the love that I hold inside.

El Condor Pasa (If I Could)

I'd rather be a sparrow than a snail.
Yes I would.
If I could,
I surely would.

I'd rather be a hammer than a nail.
Yes I would.
If I only could,
I surely would.

Away, I'd rather sail away
Like a swan that's here and gone.
A man gets tied up to the ground,
He gives the world its saddest sound,
Its saddest sound.

I'd rather be a forest than a street.
Yes I would.
If I could,
I surely would.

I'd rather feel the earth beneath my feet
Yes I would.
If I only could,
I surely would.

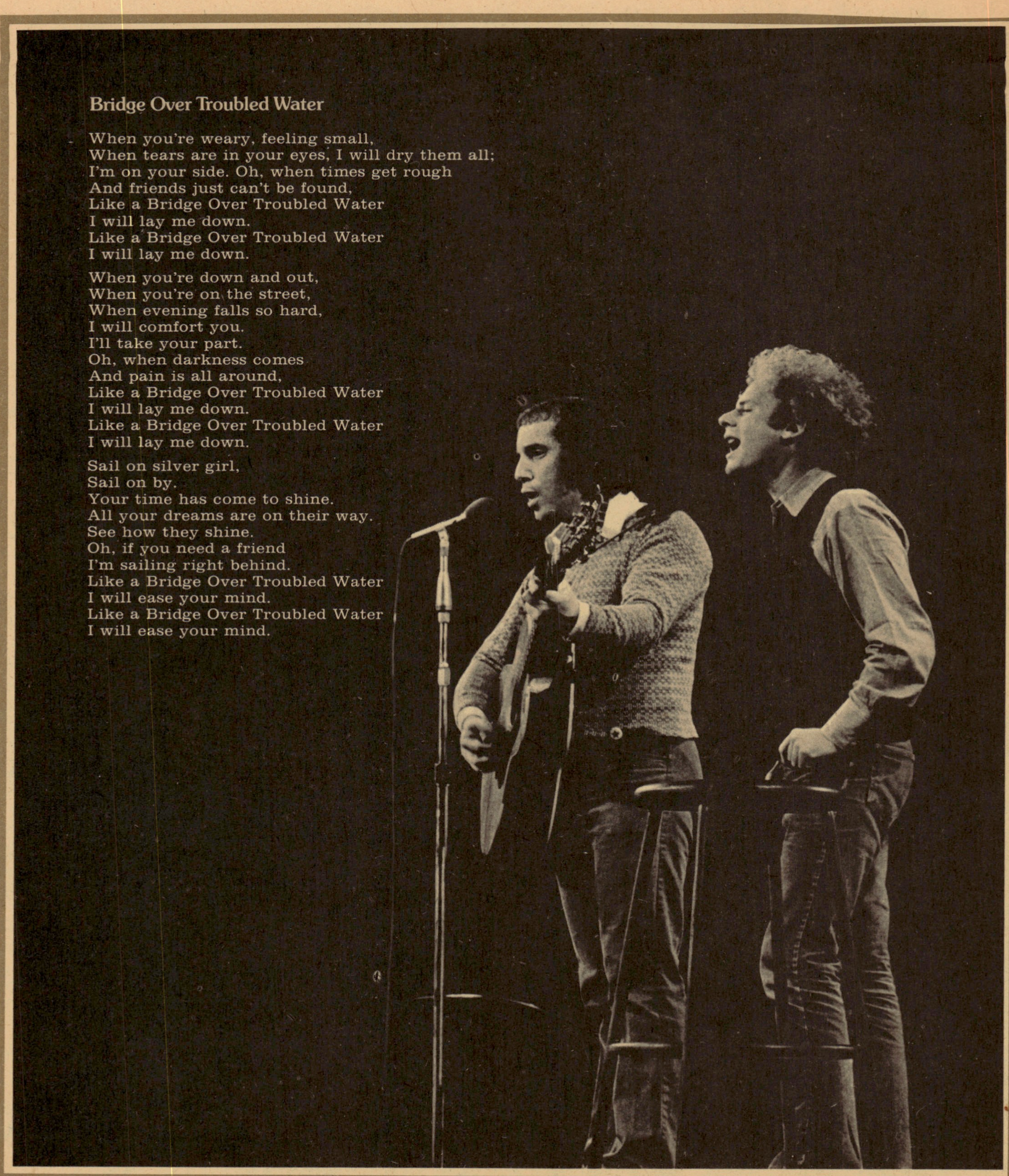

Bridge Over Troubled Water

When you're weary, feeling small,
When tears are in your eyes, I will dry them all;
I'm on your side. Oh, when times get rough
And friends just can't be found,
Like a Bridge Over Troubled Water
I will lay me down.
Like a Bridge Over Troubled Water
I will lay me down.

When you're down and out,
When you're on the street,
When evening falls so hard,
I will comfort you.
I'll take your part.
Oh, when darkness comes
And pain is all around,
Like a Bridge Over Troubled Water
I will lay me down.
Like a Bridge Over Troubled Water
I will lay me down.

Sail on silver girl,
Sail on by.
Your time has come to shine.
All your dreams are on their way.
See how they shine.
Oh, if you need a friend
I'm sailing right behind.
Like a Bridge Over Troubled Water
I will ease your mind.
Like a Bridge Over Troubled Water
I will ease your mind.

WINNING COMBINATION FOR GRAMMY AWARDS

Arthur Garfunkel, left, and Paul Simon are laden down with Grammy's after they carried off major honors at presentation ceremonies in Hollywood. The 'Oscars' of the recording business were given to the pair's 'Bridge Over Troubled Water' as the best record and best album of the year. Simon holds additional Grammy for writing the song which was a also judged best contemporary song. (Story on B-6)

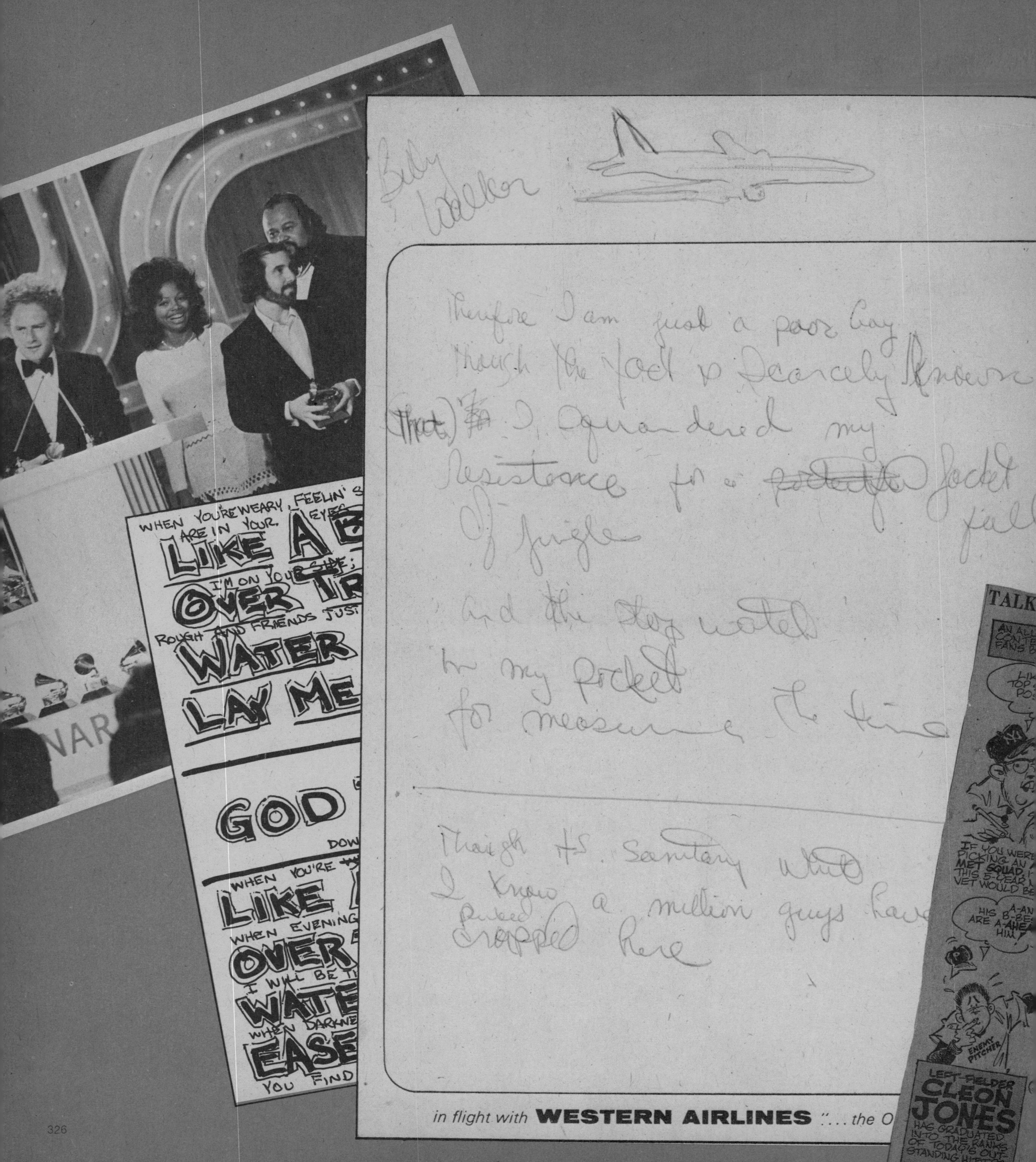
NAR
WHEN YOU'RE WEARY, FEELIN'
ARE IN YOUR EYES
LIKE A
I'M ON YOUR SIDE;
OVER
ROUGH AND FRIENDS JUST
WATER
LAY ME
GOD
WHEN YOU'RE
LIKE
WHEN EVENING
OVER
I WILL BE
WHEN DARKNE
EASE
YOU FIND
Billy Walker
Therefore I am just a poor boy
Though the story's scarcely known
(That) I squandered my
Resistance for a pocket full
Of jingles
And the stag watch
In my pocket
For measuring the time
Though it's sanitary white
I know a million guys have
puked
dropped here
in flight with WESTERN AIRLINES "... the O
TALK
IF YOU WERE PICKING AN
MET SQUAD,
THIS 5-YEAR
VET WOULD BE
ENEMY PITCHER
LEFT-FIELDER CLEON JONES
HAS GRADUATED INTO THE RANKS OF TODAY'S OUT-STANDING HITTERS.

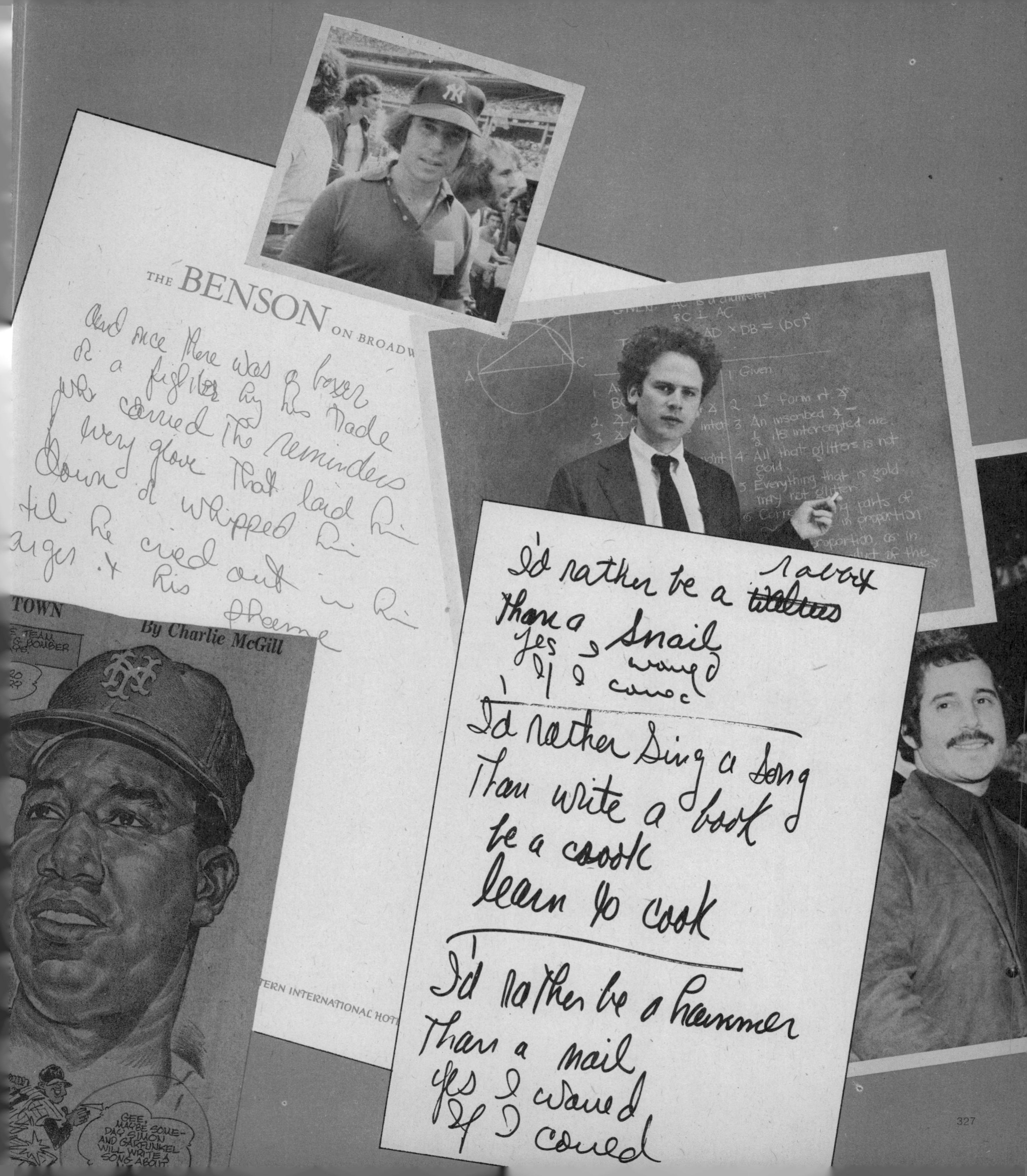
THE BENSON ON BROADW
And once there was a boxer
or a fighter by his trade
who carried the reminders
every glove that laid him
down and whipped him
til he cried out in his
anger & his shame
TOWN
By Charlie McGill
TERN INTERNATIONAL HOT
GEE, MAYBE SOME-DAY SIMON AND GARFUNKEL WILL WRITE A SONG ABOUT
1 Given
All that glitters is not gold
Everything that is gold may not glitter
I'd rather be a sparrow
Than a snail
Yes I would
If I could
I'd rather sing a song
Than write a book
be a crook
learn to cook
I'd rather be a hammer
Than a nail
Yes I would
If I could

PAUL SIMON

Mother And Child Reunion

No, I would not give you false hope
On this strange and mournful day,
But the Mother And Child Reunion
Is only a motion away,

Oh, little darling of mine.
I can't for the life of me
Remember a sadder day,
I know they say let it be,
But it just don't work out that way,
And the course of a lifetime runs over
and over again.

No, I would not give you false hope
On this strange and mournful day,
When the Mother And Child Reunion
Is only a motion away,

Oh, little darling of mine.
I just can't believe it's so,
And though it seems strange to say,
I never been laid so low
In such a mysterious way,
And the course of a lifetime runs over
and over again.

But I would not give you false hope
On this strange and mournful day,
When the Mother And Child Reunion
Is only a motion away,
Oh, oh the Mother And Child Reunion
Is only a motion away,
Oh, the Mother And Child Reunion
Is only a moment away.

Duncan

Couple in the next room bound to win a prize,
They've been going at it all night long,
Well, I'm trying to get some sleep,
But these motel walls are cheap,
Lincoln Duncan is my name and here's my song,
Here's my song.

My father was a fisherman,
My mama was the fisherman's friend,
And I was born in the boredom
and the chowder,
So when I reached my prime,
I left my home in the Maritimes,
Headed down the turnpike for New England,
Sweet New England.

Holes in my confidence, holes in the
knees of my jeans,
I was left without a penny in my pocket,
Oo hoo hoo wee,
I's about destituted as a kid could be,
And I wished I wore a ring so I could hock it,
I'd like to hock it.

A young girl in a parking lot
Was preaching to a crowd,
Singing sacred songs and reading from the Bible.
Well, I told her I was lost,
And she told me all about the Pentecost,
And I seen that girl as the road to my survival.

Just later on the very same night
When I crept to her tent with a flashlight,
And my long years of innocence ended,
Well, she took me to the woods, saying,
"Here comes something and it feels so good!"
And just like a dog I was befriended,
I was befriended.

Oh, oh, what a night,
Oh, what a garden of delight,
Even now that sweet memory lingers,
I was playing my guitar,
Lying underneath the stars,
Just thanking the Lord for my fingers,
For my fingers.

Everything Put Together Falls Apart

Paraphernalia never hides
your broken bones,
And I don't know why you want to try,
It's plain to see you're on your own.
Uh huh, I ain't blind, no,
Some folks are crazy,
Others walk that border line.
Watch what you're doing,
Taking downs to get off to sleep,
And ups to start you on your way;
After a while they'll change your style,
Mm, I see it happening ev'ry day.
Uh huh, spare your heart.
Ev'rything put together
Sooner or later falls apart,
There's nothing to it, nothing to it.
You can cry and you can lie,
For all the good it'll do you, you can die,
Oh, but when it's done and the police come,
And they lay you down for dead,
Uh huh, just remember what I said!

Run That Body Down

Went to my doctor yesterday.
She said I seem to be O.K.
She said, "Paul, you better look around.
How long you think that you can Run
That Body Down?
How many nights you think that you can do
what you been doing?
Who now, who you fooling?"
I came back home and I went into bed.
Ah, I was resting my head.
My wife came in and she said,
"What's wrong, sweet boy, what's wrong?"
Ah, I told her what's wrong.
I said, "Peg, you better look around.
How long you think that you can Run
That Body Down?
How many nights you think that you can do
what you been doing?
Who now, who you fooling?
Who now, you fooling?"

Armistice Day

On Armistice Day
The Philharmonic will play,
But the songs that we sing will be sad.
Shuffling brown tunes,
Hanging around, ahoo.
No long-drawn blown-out excuses were made,
When I needed a friend, she was there,
Just like an easy chair.
Oo Oo
Mm
Armistice Day, Armistice Day,

That's all I really wanted to say.
Oh, I'm weary from waiting in Washington, D.C.
I'm coming to see my congressman,
but he's avoiding me.
Weary from waiting down in Washington, D.C.

Oh, congresswoman, won't you
tell that congressman,
I've waited such a long time,
I've about waited all I can.
Oh, congresswoman, won't you
tell that congressman.

Me And Julio Down By The Schoolyard

The mama pajama rolled out of bed,
And she ran to the police station,
When the papa found out, he began to shout,
And he started the investigation.
It's against the law, it was against the law,
What the mama saw, it was against the law.
The mama looked down and spit on the ground
Ev'ry time my name gets mentioned,
The papa said, "Oy, if I get that boy
I'm gonna stick him in the house of detention."
Well, I'm on my way,
I don't know where I'm going,
I'm on my way,
I'm taking my time but I don't know where.
Goodbye to Rosie, the Queen of Corona,
See you, Me And Julio Down
By The Schoolyard.
See you, Me And Julio Down
By The Schoolyard.

In a couple of days they come and
take me away,
But the press let the story leak,
And when the radical priest come to
get me released,
We was all on the cover of **Newsweek**.
Well, I'm on my way,
I don't know where I'm going,
I'm on my way,
I'm taking my time but I don't knew where.
Goodbye to Rosie, the Queen of Corona,
See you, Me And Julio Down
By The Schoolyard.
See you, Me And Julio Down
By The Schoolyard.
See you, Me And Julio Down
By The Schoolyard.

Peace Like A River

Ah, Peace Like A River ran through the city,
Long past the midnight curfew we
sat starry-eyed,
Oh, oh, we were satisfied.

And I remember misinformation followed
us like a plague,
Nobody knew from time to time if the
plans were changed,
Oh, oh, oh, if the plans were changed.
You can beat us with wires, You can
beat us with chain,
You can run out your rules, but you know you
can't outrun the history train.

I seen a glorious day, ai ee ee ee.

Ah, four in the morning I woke up from out
of my dreams,
Nowhere to go but back to sleep,
but I'm reconciled,
Oh, oh, oh, I'm gonna be up for awhile.
Oh, oh, oh, I'm gonna be up for awhile.
Oh, oh, oh, I'm gonna be up for awhile.

Papa Hobo

Mm It's carbon and monoxide,
The ole Detroit perfume,
It hangs on the highways in the morning,
And it lays you down by noon.
Oh, Papa Hobo,
You can see that I'm dressed like a schoolboy,
But I feel like a clown,
It's a nat'ral reaction I learned in
this basketball town.

Sweep up,
I been sweepin' up the tips I've made.
I been living on Gatorade,
Planning my getaway.

Detroit, Detroit,
Got a hell of a hockey team,
Got a left-handed way of making a man
Sign up on that automotive dream,
Oh yeah, oh yeah.
Oh, Papa, Papa Hobo, could you slip me a ride?

Well, it's just after breakfast,
I'm in the road and the weatherman lied.

Paranoia Blues

I've got some so-called friends,
They'll smile right to my face,
But, when my back is turned,
They'd like to stick it to me, yes, they would.
Oh, no, no,
Oh, no, no.
There's only one thing I need to know:
Whose side are you on?

I fly into J.F.K.
My heart goes boom boom boom.
I know that customs man,
He's gonna take me to that little room.
Oh, no, no,
Oh, no, no.
There's only one thing I need to know:
Whose side are you on, whose side are you on?

I got the Paranoia Blues from knocking around
in New York City,
Where they roll you for a nickel, and they stick
you for the extra dime.
Any way you choose, you're bound to lose in
New York City,
Oh, I just got out in the nick of time.
Well, I just got out in the nick of time.

Once I was down in Chinatown,
I was eating some Lin's chow fon,
I happened to turn around,
And when I looked I seen my chow fon's gone.
Oh, no, no,
Oh, no, no.
There's only one thing I need to know:
Whose side are you on, whose side are you on?
Well, there's only one thing I need to know:
Whose side, whose side, whose side?

Congratulations

Congratulations!
Oh, seems like you've done it again,
And I ain't had such misery
Since I don't know when,
Oh, and I don't know when,
Oh, and I don't know when.

I notice so many people slipping away,
And many more waiting in the lines
In the courtrooms today,
Oh, in the courtrooms today.

Love is not a game, love is not a toy,
Love's no romance.

Love will do you in, and love will wash you out,
And needless to say
You won't stand a chance,
And you won't stand a chance.

I'm hungry for learning,
Won't you answer me, please.
Can a man and a woman
Live together in peace,
Oh, live together in peace?